Repentance

KINOfiles Film Companions
General Editor: Richard Taylor

Written for cineastes and students alike, KINOfiles are readable, authoritative, illustrated companion handbooks to the most important and interesting films to emerge from Russian cinema from its beginnings to the present. Each KINOfile investigates the production, context and reception of the film and the people who made it, and analyses the film itself and its place in Russian and World cinema. KINOfiles will also include films of the other countries that once formed part of the Soviet Union, as well as works by émigré filmmakers working in the Russian tradition.

KINOfiles form a part of KINO: The Russian Cinema Series.

The Battleship Potemkin
Richard Taylor

Bed and Sofa
Julian Graffy

Burnt by the Sun
Birgit Beumers

The Cranes are Flying
Josephine Woll

Ivan the Terrible
Joan Neuberger

Little Vera
Frank Beardow

The Man with the Movie Camera
Graham Roberts

Mirror
Natasha Synessios

Repentance
Josephine Woll and Denise Youngblood

The Sacrifice
Christine Åkesson

REPENTANCE

JOSEPHINE WOLL AND
DENISE J. YOUNGBLOOD

KINOfile Film Companion 4

I.B.Tauris *Publishers*
LONDON • NEW YORK

Published in 2001 by I.B.Tauris & Co Ltd
6 Salem Road, London W2 4BU
175 Fifth Avenue, New York NY 10010
www.ibtauris.com

In the United States of America and in Canada distributed by
St Martins Press, 175 Fifth Avenue, New York NY 10010

ISBN 1 86064 395 7

A full CIP record for this book is available from the British Library
A full CIP record for this book is available from the Library of Congress

Library of Congress catalog card: available

Typeset in Monotype Calisto by the Midlands Book Typesetting Company,
Loughborough, Leicestershire
Printed and bound in Great Britain by MPG Books Ltd, Bodmin, Cornwall

Contents

List of Illustrations

Acknowledgements

We would like to thank Birgit Beumers, Julian Graffy, and Graham Roberts for their comments on an earlier version—and especially Richard Taylor, who has been both helpful and patient.

We are grateful for permission to reproduce the following stills: Figs. 1, 4, 5, 6, 8, 13, 14, 17, 18, 19, 21, 23 courtesy Museum of Modern Art, New York. Figs. 2, 3, 7, 10, 11, 15, 16, 20, 22 courtesy Cannon Film Group. Figs. 9, 12 courtesy Richard Taylor.

All translations are our own unless otherwise noted.

Note on Transliteration

Transliteration from the Cyrillic to the Latin alphabet is a perennial problem for writers on Russian subjects. We have opted for a dual system: in the text we have used the Library of Congress system (without diacritics), but we have broken from this system (a) when a Russian name has a clear English version (e.g. Maria instead of Mariia, Alexander instead of Aleksandr); (b) when a Russian name has an accepted English spelling, or when Russian names are of Germanic origin (e.g. Yeltsin instead of Eltsin; Eisenstein instead of Eizenshtein); (c) when a Russian surname ends in -ii or -yi this is replaced by a single -y (e.g. Dostoevsky instead of Dostoevskii), and all Christian names end in a single -i; (d) when 'ia' or 'iu' are voiced (at the beginning of a word and when preceded by a vowel) they are rendered as 'ya' or 'yu' (e.g. Daneliya, Yuri)—with the sole addition of the name Asya to avoid confusion with the continent, Asia. In the scholarly apparatus we have adhered to the Library of Congress system (with diacritics) for the specialist.

And art made tongue-tied by authority
And folly, doctor-like, controlling skill,
And simple truth miscall'd simplicity
And captive good attending captain ill,

William Shakespeare
Sonnet 66

Credits

English Title: REPENTANCE
Georgian Title: MONANIEBA
Russian Title: POKAIANIE

Release: 1986, color, 151 minutes, Georgian with English subtitles
Director: Tengiz Abuladze
Producer: Gruziafilm

Cast

Avtandil Makharadze	Varlam Aravidze and Abel Aravidze
Zeinab Botsvadze	Keti Barateli
Ia Ninidze	Guliko Aravidze
Merab Ninidze	Tornike Aravidze
Ketevan Abuladze	Nino Barateli
Edisher Giorgiobani	Sandro Barateli
Kakhi Kavsadze	Mikhail Korisheli
Nino Zakariadze	Elena Korisheli
Veriko Anzhaparidze	Old Woman

Scenarists: Nana Djanelidze, Tengiz Abuladze, Rezo Kveselava
Cinematographer: Mikhail Agranovich
Production Designer: Georgi Mikeladze
Music Coordinator: Nana Djanelidze
UK Distributors: Cannon Film Distribution
US Distributors: The Cannon Group; Media Home Entertainment (video)

Introduction: 'The First Swallow of Perestroika'[1]

In 1987, the Russian words *glasnost* and *perestroika* entered the English language, thanks to the sweeping reforms launched in the Soviet Union by its new Party Secretary, Mikhail Gorbachev. Nowhere were the effects of glasnost and perestroika more apparent than in the arts, especially the cinema. This was, after all, a society in which art, as the epigraph notes, had been 'made tongue-tied by authority'. The Union of Cinematographers quickly 'came out' for Gorbachev—and became one of his most important early supporters. Over a two-year period several dozen banned films came 'off the shelf' for public release.[2]

By autumn 1986, Mikhail Gorbachev had been in power some 18 months. He and his cultural commissar Alexander Yakovlev devised their twin policies of glasnost and perestroika in order to achieve a significant overhaul of the floundering, foundering Soviet economy. Glasnost would be the carrot with which to lure the Soviet intelligentsia into supporting perestroika, and would, as well, seduce back into civic participation the alienated youth of the country.[3] After a slow start in spring 1986, by October of that year the tide of glasnost was steadily creeping up the beach of the Soviet press, measured in weekly, sometimes daily increments.

Gorbachev and Yakovlev found their natural allies among the *shestidesiatniki*, the men and women of the Sixties who had come of age during Khrushchev's tenure as Party Secretary: people like the poet Yevgeny Yevtushenko and the poet and journalist Vitaly Korotich, who became the new editor of the weekly satiric magazine *Ogonek*; people like Grigory Baklanov and Sergei Zalygin, whom Gorbachev appointed to edit, respectively, the prestigious 'thick' monthlies *Znamia* and *Novyi mir*.

Khrushchev had propelled the process of de-Stalinization, most notably with his speeches at the Twentieth and Twenty-Second Party Congresses (1956 and 1962), but for many reasons had left office with that particular agenda, among numerous others, unfinished. These 'sons of Khrushchev', mostly liberal intellectuals, wanted to finish the job he had begun, by exposing Stalin's crimes and by publishing works suppressed under Stalin or afterwards.

First they resurrected ghosts and readmitted exiles. *Ogonek* published hitherto taboo poetry by Nikolai Gumilev, shot in August 1921 for alleged counter-revolutionary activity, and a few of Vladimir Nabokov's poems. By November 1986, readers queued up at kiosks to buy out their supply of *Ogonek*, eagerly scanning its table of contents with equal parts of hope—what now?—and trepidation that censorship might have been reimposed, blocking further revelations. They scrutinized the back covers of *Novyi mir* and *Znamia*, where the contents of future issues were listed, and found astounding promises: Solzhenitsyn and Pasternak, Grossman and Zamiatin, writers whose works, if not their very names, had been banned from Soviet periodicals for years and sometimes decades. Throughout that winter and the following spring readers rediscovered both a lost culture and a lost history, in works as different as Anna Akhmatova's great poem of the Terror, *Requiem*, and Anatoly Rybakov's long-suppressed novel, *Children of the Arbat*.

The same recuperative process characterized the film industry. At the Fifth Congress of the Union of Cinematographers, in May 1986, a new guard had swept away the stultifying policies of the former leadership. Two days later its newly-elected First Secretary, Elem Klimov, created a Conflict Commission to 'review the inventory of banned films, and to decide on controversial new ones'.[4] The Commission viewed over 100 shelved films of every sort; all were eventually released. By 1987 audiences finally had the chance to see Klimov's 1975 film about the Romanovs, *Agonia* (released in the USA as *Rasputin*); Aleksei German's 1971 *Roadcheck* [*Proverka na dorogakh*, also known as *Trials on the Road*], about a Soviet soldier who, as a former POW, is suspected of collaborating with the Nazis; and Alexander Askoldov's first and last film, *Commissar* (1968).

Repentance, the movie that came to symbolize the glasnost era for Soviet citizens, was not, however, one of these banned films that had just come off 'the shelf'. The well-known Georgian director Tengiz Abuladze, who had established an international reputation with *The

Prayer [*Molba*] and *The Tree of Desire* [*Drevo zhelania*, sometimes translated as *The Wishing Tree*] was able to complete the third film of his historical trilogy, *Repentance* [*Pokaianie*], with the help of a powerful patron, Eduard Shevardnadze, then head of Georgia's Communist Party, and later well-known in the West as Gorbachev's polished and accomplished Foreign Minister and as President of the post-Soviet Republic of Georgia.

We first saw *Repentance* at this heady moment in Soviet cultural history, Josephine Woll in Moscow at Dom Kino, the centre of the Cinematographers' Union, in November 1986 and Denise Youngblood a few months later at one of the film's first US screenings, at the University of California, Berkeley in early 1987. A continent apart, the circumstances were remarkably similar. Crowds gathered for hours before the screening, hoping for a good seat—or *any* seat. The air was charged with anticipation, and hundreds of excited and emotional people packed the theaters, but dead silence fell as the film began. For the next 2½ hours, not a sound came from the audience, despite the discomfort of overcrowded theaters, and despite the amusement that native Russian-speakers felt at the fact that the print was one that had been dubbed into Russian. (The juxtaposition of the Russian language and the obviously Georgian faces, expressions, and gestures of the actors were jarring to many in the audience.) As the final credits rolled, there was a momentary hush, and then wild applause broke out. It was truly a cultural 'moment', one that we shall never forget.

It is not easy, however, to separate the movie from the moment. As stunning as *Repentance* is in many respects, it is also long, slow, difficult and irritating for some viewers, whether Western or Soviet. Assessing reception is always problematic, especially when a film, like *Repentance*, is a 'must see' event, a movie that people feel obligated to view and support as a kind of political or intellectual statement. This definitely appears to be the case in the Soviet context, as Soviet critic Tatiana Khloplyankina explicitly acknowledged when she wrote, shortly after the film opened for unrestricted screenings in Moscow in January 1987: 'The release of *Repentance* (1984) is one of those big events that certify that the order of our life is happily and inevitably changing.' She added: 'It is indeed a work of art. *But first of all it is a fact of our current social life*' [emphasis added].[5] Not surprisingly, director Abuladze waxed more poetic. 'After showings in every city,' he told critic Karen

Rosenberg in an interview, 'people got up and applauded the blank screen. It was the first swallow of perestroika.'[6]

Likewise, the Western art-film crowd felt morally obligated to see *Repentance* and all the formerly banned Soviet films circulating in Europe and the USA during the late Eighties. Privately, however, many American film scholars confided to us that they felt most of these movies fell short of Western film-making standards and received acclaim mainly because of the Western cultural elite's sympathetic support for the travails of Soviet artists. Similarly, professional Slavicists felt obliged to see the glasnost-era films, and with the exception of those scholars specifically interested in the arts, many found these late Soviet pictures 'boring'. In the USA, distributors agreed, and very few of these movies were commercially distributed. *Repentance* was the rare exception.

Now more than a decade has passed, and the cheering has stopped. With the collapse of the Soviet Union and the infrastructure that had supported it, the once substantial Soviet film industry—now in its Russian guise—is still in the complex process of reinventing itself. Nor have the studios in any of the former republics fared better. The Georgian film industry, one of the oldest and proudest in the former empire, is struggling to survive, not surprising given the years of civil war in Georgia following independence. The disappearance of its spiritual leader certainly has not helped: Tengiz Abuladze died unexpectedly in 1994, at the age of 70, of a heart attack. *Repentance*, his triumph, also turned out to be his last film.

How well has *Repentance* aged? It remains original, even audacious, in its conception and style, a fact Western and Soviet critics immediately recognized and acknowledged. Abuladze referred to it as a 'phantasmagoria' in the tradition of Georgian folklore (a tradition that is reminiscent of the 'magical realism' of Latin American literature.)[7] *Repentance* is an important historical artefact, one that, like its literary counterpart *Children of the Arbat*, remains central to an understanding of the cultural revolution that rocked the final years of Soviet power. It is, therefore, an intrinsic part of history. Few movies can claim that stature.

But does *Repentance* merit its own companion guide in a series such as this? Does *Repentance*, so long, slow and difficult, deserve its place in the pantheon of immortal Soviet movies like *Potemkin* that have indelibly marked the history of film art? Since its release, we have convinced dozens of rather unlikely viewers—American university students—that *Repentance* is indeed a movie worth watching, again and again. We hope to demonstrate the many reasons why in the following pages.

Notes

1 Tengiz Abuladze on *Repentance*; quoted by Karen Rosenberg in 'Movies in the Soviet Union', *The Nation*, 21 November 1988, p. 526.

2 This story is well told in Andrew Horton and Michael Brashinsky, *The Zero Hour: Glasnost and Soviet Cinema in Transition* (Princeton, NJ: Princeton University Press, 1992, and in Anna Lawton, *Kinoglasnost: Soviet Cinema in Our Time*, Cambridge: Cambridge University Press, 1992).

3 John Dunlop, 'Soviet Cultural Politics', *Problems of Communism*, 1987, (November–December), p. 35.

4 Lawton, *Kinoglasnost*, p. 57.

5 Tatiana Khloplyankina, 'On the Road That Leads to the Truth', in Michael Brashinsky and Andrew Horton, *Russian Critics on the Cinema of Glasnost*, (Cambridge: Cambridge University Press, 1994), p. 51. This article originally appeared in *Moskovskaia pravda*, 4 February 1987.

6 Rosenberg, 'Movies in the Soviet Union', p. 526.

7 Horton and Brashinsky, *Zero Hour*, pp. 40–1; Lawton, *Kinoglasnost*, p. 156. The source is Alla Gerber's account of her two interviews with Abuladze, published in *Sovetskii fil m* in 1987.

1. 'The Content of the Form': Plot and Structure

The plot and structure of *Repentance*, with its two framing stories and long flashback, are extremely complicated. Reminiscent of the *matryoshka*, the Russian nested doll, *Repentance* is a story within a story within a story. Unraveling these intertwined tales is an essential first step to understanding what the formalist critic Viktor Shklovsky called the *siuzhet* or 'plot-theme' of the film. It is certainly intrinsic to any attempt to interpret the movie and its multiplicity of meanings. To paraphrase Hayden White, *Repentance*'s form definitely holds the key to its content. It is, therefore, particularly important to establish the sequence of events as plots and subplots unfold.[1]

The First Framing Story

Repentance opens with a dream-like prologue: a woman is in her kitchen decorating an elaborate cake while a man sits at the table reading the newspaper. He exclaims over the obituary of a recently deceased mayor of their town, one Varlam Aravidze (whose surname means 'everyman' or 'any man' in the Georgian language).[2] The woman appears distinctly uninterested in this news and puts the finishing touches on her cake. Although the viewer cannot know it until the end of the film, this scene, which initially appears to be only tenuously related to what follows, is critical, rather than tangential. It launches the film's first framing story.

The Second Framing Story

The next scene, which represents the beginning of the second framing story, is set at the funeral of the so-called 'great man',

Varlam Aravidze. In a manner reminiscent of Fellini's comic surrealism, a highly stylized group of mourners stands around Aravidze's flower-draped coffin. They wipe a glycerin tear or two from their eyes and utter a few stock phrases of comfort to the deceased's family. A tiny, gnome-like man, whom everyone present seems to fear, reads a long hortatory poem, and the mourners suddenly break into rousing song.

We then follow the coffin as it is slowly carried outdoors to the cemetery. After the interment, the dead man's family, consisting of his son Abel, his daughter-in-law Guliko, and his teenaged grandson Tornike, walk slowly away, arm in arm, seemingly the perfect family. Nothing in this film is, however, what it appears to be.

That evening, Abel and Guliko are in their bedroom preparing for sleep. They are anything but a loving couple: Guliko taunts her husband for being a 'poor little orphan' now that his father has passed away. With bitter mockery, her face slathered with cold cream, she asks him why his mistress did not attend the funeral. Abel pleads with her to leave him alone. Going to the window to investigate why their dog is wildly barking, Guliko sees a horrifying sight: Varlam's corpse is propped against a tree in the courtyard of their rather palatial home. The family quickly reburies Varlam, but early the next morning, as Guliko cautiously looks out of her window, she faces precisely the same outrage: Varlam's dead body leaning against the tree.

It is time to call the police, who bustle about like the Soviet equivalent of the Keystone Cops, announcing that they must take the corpse into custody (for disturbing the peace, we might assume). The cops unceremoniously dump Varlam into the back of a Black Maria. But Varlam will not rest, even though the gate to the cemetery has now been locked and chained against intruders. The corpse next reappears slumped on a bench, the chain from the cemetery gate wound around its neck.

The Aravidze men and the police decide to spend the night guarding the grave, hoping to catch the miscreant. As it turns out, only Varlam's grandson Tornike really cares about the fate of the old man. Abel and the chief of police head off to a feast at a neighboring dignitary's house; the two cops left behind are joking and drinking behind a headstone. So it is left to Tornike to hear the rustling of the grave-robber, and he shoots and captures the shadowy figure.

If it were not already clear that this film is no ordinary family melodrama, it is now. The desecrator of Varlam's grave is not a man, as Tornike and everyone else have assumed, but a woman. Indeed, she is the red-haired cake baker from the movie's opening scene. Her name is Keti Barateli. At her trial, Keti theatrically dresses in white with a magnificent white-plumed hat. She defiantly announces that '... as long as I am alive, Varlam will not rest. The sentence is final'. She then proceeds to tell her story, a story that transforms her trial for grave robbery into a trial of something much more serious: the trial of Varlam Aravidze for his crimes against humanity.

The Flashback

Keti's long narrative flashback lasts for some 75 minutes, about half the film's length. This flashback easily stands alone as a self-contained parable of the terror of the Soviet Thirties. Keti, now a middle-aged woman, first saw Varlam when she was an eight-year-old child, shortly after he was first elected mayor of their town. She is the daughter of Sandro Barateli, a famous artist of ancient lineage, who quickly establishes himself as an opponent of the new order. Sandro first attracts Varlam's malevolent eye when he prevents Keti from watching Varlam's inauguration parade. Sandro further confirms Varlam's suspicions when he joins two elderly 'blue-bloods' with the Jewish names Moise and Miriam in opposing the government's continued use of a medieval church as a scientific laboratory for sound experiments. (This scene appears to cast god-fearing people, of whatever religious affiliation, against the godless.) When the trio's mild and reasoned protest about the importance of historical preservation results in Moise's and Miriam's arrest, Sandro immediately lodges a complaint with his old friend Mikhail Korisheli, the local Party chief. Korisheli, an austere but principled revolutionary, successfully intercedes with Varlam to obtain their release.

One night shortly thereafter, Varlam decides to pay the Baratelis a surprise visit, ostensibly to apologize for the false arrest of the frightened old couple. Varlam appears at their antique- and painting-filled apartment, accompanied by his henchmen Doksopoulo and Riktafelov, and his young son, Abel. Sandro and Varlam discuss art, specifically Sandro's work, which has impressed Varlam with its beauty. Then Sandro, his lovely wife Nino, and their guest, Elena Korisheli, wife of the Party chief, listen to Varlam, Doksopoulo and Riktafelov sing *bel canto* with skill and gusto. As an encore, Varlam chooses not to sing, but instead recites Shakespeare's Sonnet 66 ('Tired with all these for restful death I cry').

Meanwhile Abel and Keti, who are about the same age, are in another room, discussing a weighty spiritual matter: whether Abel's dead mother is in heaven, as Keti believes. Keti's mother Nino (and all Georgians know that St Nino brought Christianity to Georgia more than 1500 years ago) reassures Abel. The uninvited guests depart as suddenly as they arrived, but even more unexpectedly, by jumping out of the second-storey window and galloping away on waiting horses. Varlam, however, returns briefly, to give Nino the crucifix that Abel has taken from the house.

Later that night, Doksopoulo and Riktafelov reappear, now clad in knightly armor, to arrest Sandro. The Terror has begun, not only for the Baratelis, but for everyone. Mikhail Korisheli is arrested soon after, followed by Elena Korisheli, a 'truckload of [people named] Darbaiseli' that Doksopoulo has rounded up to fulfil his arrest quota, and finally, Nino Barateli. 'And that was the end of Nino Barateli'. Keti never saw either of her parents again. For this, and so much more, Varlam must never rest.

Return to the Second Framing Story

At the end of Keti's tragic discourse about the fate of her family in those 'forgotten' times, the courtroom, packed with supporters of the Aravidzes, erupts in fury. 'She's insane!' they shout. Profoundly affected by Keti's story is young Tornike Aravidze, who adored his grandfather and is the only one present who truly knew nothing about his terrible past. Tornike sits beside his parents, stunned, lost in a daydream in which an aged and deranged Varlam is locked in a tower, mortally afraid of sunlight, yet defiantly and arrogantly challenging its life-giving powers. Coming back to himself, he assaults his father, Abel, with questions: did Abel know? Abel defends his own father, Varlam, feebly, with formulaic responses: 'the situation was different then'; Varlam 'never personally killed anybody', etc. Tornike is not comforted by these relativistic blandishments, the stock-in-trade of the twentieth century's perpetrators and their collaborators.

Back at the Aravidze compound, while Abel and Guliko plot with their political cohorts to manipulate the outcome of the case by having Keti declared insane and committed to an asylum, Tornike has another, even more disturbing daydream. He sees his mother, Guliko, as yet another amoral and unfeeling collaborator, dancing provocatively around Varlam's corpse, her lips curled in her characteristic sneer. Abel, too, is losing his emotional equilibrium. Although he readily agrees to Guliko's plans regarding Keti, Abel spends the night in their cellar. There, in a scene recalling Hamlet and his father's ghost, Abel converses with an apparition, who is eventually revealed to be Varlam's completely unrepentant ghost. The apparition, shrouded in shadows, is eating a raw fish (possibly symbolizing the body of Christ?) with revolting gusto; in the words of Anna Lawton, it is 'a profane rite of Communion—a veritable Black Mass.'[3] We also gradually discern through the darkness that the damp cellar is filled with moldering paintings, all that remains of Sandro Barateli's art.

Predictably, the Aravidzes' scheme succeeds. Keti is declared insane and sentenced to an asylum, but of the Aravidze clan, only Guliko truly rejoices. Abel sits beside her, stunned, holding the skeleton of the fish that the ghost of the previous evening had been gobbling when they had their metaphysical conversation about the nature of good and evil in the cellar. Abel's growing doubts about his own sanity (after his encounter with Varlam's ghost) are confirmed by Keti's defiant last words to the court: 'Aravidze is not dead. He's alive and continues to corrupt society.'

Although the film's pace has been to this point quite leisurely, it picks up speed dramatically as it rushes to its tragic conclusion. The distraught boy Tornike visits Keti in her cell, begging her forgiveness, before returning home to confront his father once again. He screams at Abel: 'How can you go on lying forever?' and rushes to his room, locking the door. Although Guliko is at the moment welcoming guests to their victory party, she alone has a premonition of the disaster about to befall them. As Guliko frantically calls out to her son and pounds helplessly on his door, Tornike shoots himself with the rifle his beloved grandfather had given him. Mad with grief, Abel Aravidze finally understands what he must do: he unearths Varlam's corpse and throws it over a cliff to the scavengers. Varlam must never lie in the consecrated ground of his native land. He is one of the 'undead'.

The First Framing Story Revisited

Abel's throwing of Varlam to the ravens is a fitting conclusion, a model of poetic (or cinematic) justice. But the film is not over; Abuladze does not want the viewer to rest either. The final scene returns us to the beginning, to the woman (who looks like Keti Barateli) calmly baking her cakes. Her companion is seated at the kitchen table as he was at the very beginning of the film, still reading Varlam's obituary. An ancient woman taps at Keti's window with a question: 'Does this road lead to a church?' Keti regards her solemnly: 'This is Varlam Street. It will not lead you to a church.' The old woman responds indignantly, 'What good is a road if it doesn't lead you to a church?' and walks slowly away, as Keti watches. Has virtually the entire film—the second framing story *and* the flashback—been no more than a moment of Keti's wishful thinking? Most viewers and critics believe so.

This vexing question cannot be answered by analysis of plot and structure alone—if indeed it can ever be answered at all. None of the three narratives, as we have seen through this synopsis, is overtly realistic. The content of each of the three tales is deliberately mystifying and frequently surrealistic. The convoluted chronological disjunctures also lay the foundations for the film's surrealism. This surrealism, so important to any effort at interpretation of the movie, is cemented by a number of stylistic devices, the subject of Chapter 3.

Before evaluating the role of these stylistic devices, however, we turn to a frame analysis of the film. Scenes are enumerated as follows: Roman numeral I designates the prologue and first section of the film, before the flashback; Roman numeral II refers to the central flashback; Roman numeral III designates the conclusion and epilogue of the film. Within each section, Arabic numerals designate individual scenes.

Notes

1   Hayden V. White, *The Content of the Form: Narrative Discourse and Historical Representation* (Baltimore, MD: Johns Hopkins University Press, 1987).

2   Julie Christensen, 'Tengiz Abuladze's *Repentance* and the Georgian Nationalist Cause', *Slavic Review* Vol. 50, no. 1 (Spring 1991), p. 166.

3   Anna Lawton, *Kinoglasnost: Soviet Cinema in Our Time*, (Cambridge: Cambridge University Press, 1992), p. 157.

2. *Repentance*: Frame Analysis

Image	Dialogue	Sound	Commentary
I 1 Extreme close-up [ecu] of hands trimming a rose;		Guitar music (non-diegetic)	
Middle shot [ms] of a woman framed in doorway, bent over a cake she is frosting.			Immediate temporal disjunction between Keti's 'modern', man-tailored shirt and horse-drawn carriage with top-hatted driver.
A seated bearded man with newspaper on lap takes a large mouthful of cake.	Man: 'The cake is delicious, Keti.'		
Cut to woman carrying cake, decorated with a miniature cross-topped church. She passes it through open window to customer, who climbs into a horse-drawn carriage.			
Ecu of her fingers manipulating a cross on to another cake. Ms of man stuffing cake into his mouth while he speaks.	Man: 'My God! What a misfortune! We've lost a great man ... He was more than a relative, he was my closest friend. My luck is ended. Dear Varlam is gone.'		
Slow zoom in to Keti peering through her reading glasses at the paper.	Keti: 'Still, you were lucky to have known such a man.'		Allusion to Stalin's role as 'friend' to all creatures, human and animal alike.
Cut to ecu of Varlam's beaming face in newspaper photo. Slow zoom in on it.			

1   Opening scene, Keti at the bakery

I 2 Hard cut to **cu** of massed red carnations. Pan along flowers to salver with lit candles. Reverse zoom reveals four men in suits; then Varlam's powdered and pale face.	'We'll never have such a fine mayor again.' 'Why won't he be buried in the Pantheon?' 'He would have objected to it. Varlam was always a modest man.' 'No. Varlam is not dead.'	The men's clothing—black shirt, white jacket—suggest *mafiosi*. An allusion to Stalin's vaunted modesty.
Mourners file past Abel and Tornike, shaking Abel's hand. Guliko sits slightly behind and to one side of Abel. Pan of mourners' faces returns to Abel; one slips an envelope into his pocket. **Cu** of Tornike, eyes cast down.	Abel: 'Thank you, sir. I'm very grateful to you.'	
Long shot [**ls**] of coffin, banked with red carnations. Mourners step back to make room for a man almost dwarflike. Tseretelo wears white shirt and black vest. He pulls out a folded hanky to wipe his eyes; all follow suit. He reads from a prepared text. The microphone is tilted down toward him; his head is shown to reach halfway up the chests of the men standing behind him.	'Long live Tseretelo, our benefactor!' (Applause) 'We will soon commit to the earth a man of noble soul, clear mind and kind heart. . . . One dead man may be better than 1000 living ones. . . . I will single out only one of Varlam's merits, his gift for turning a friend into a foe and vice-versa. His coffin, like a *smorgasbord*, stands. . . Rest in peace, zealous toiler.'	Tseretelo is the new chief, toward whom all behave obsequiously. Disparity between physical size and power. Incongruity of language
Cu of Guliko, blotting at her dry cheeks. Tornike alone does not sing.	All sing *Samshoblo*	Song: *Samshoblo* Anthem of Georgia's national independence, May 1918–Feb. 1921

I 3 Slow pan up black surface, eventually shown to be Guliko's V-neckline. Pan up to her face; she narrows her eyes behind her glasses. The funeral procession, baskets of flowers. Final mourner holds up Varlam's portrait. Crane shot of coffin descending semi-circular staircase. At cemetery, Abel, Guliko and Tornike look their last and leave, arms linked.	Voice-over: 'He'll go, another will come into the blossoming world.' Birds twitter	Guliko hides her thoughts behind her glasses, a trait she shares with Varlam Suggestion: happy family

I 4 Night-time. Guliko smears gooey cosmetic mask on her face.	Guliko: 'Why didn't your girlfriend come to the funeral?' Abel: 'Don't be silly.'	Tinkly music; clock chimes fives times.	Contradiction: tension between Abel and Guliko
In the darkness, only her naked back, bent over Abel as if to make love to him, is visible. Portrait of Varlam watching them. Guliko hoists it on top of wardrobe. Light picks out arms entwined.	Guliko: 'My poor little orphan!' (laughs) Abel: 'Why's that portrait here?' Guliko: 'Allez-oop!'		Abel feels his father's watchful presence; Guliko can easily free herself of the burden.
Guliko goes outside to look, wearing red robe. Abel approaches a tree against which Varlam is propped, arms folded. In background, palm tree thick with clusters of fruit.	She screams.	Non-diegetic: animal howls.	Red, white and black color scheme continues.

2   Abel discovers Varlam's corpse

I 5 Reburial at night. Coffin carried at shoulder-height. Light follows pallbearers.		Night sounds: train whistle, wheels rattle, crickets, footsteps	
Guliko lies awake; again dons robe, goes to window.	Screams: 'Abel! Varlam!'		Varlam seems to be watching the investigators.
I 6 Daylight. A line of men, led by one in uniform with gun in holster, approaches Varlam. They take photographs of him. Tornike watches from balcony as the corpse, this time *sans* coffin, is loaded into paddy wagon and the barred door is locked behind.	'I'll have to arrest the corpse.' 'Ah, the times we live in— Varlam has been arrested.'	Birds twitter.	
		Clip-clop	The paddy wagon is horse-drawn: temporal disjunction.
Through an archway, Guliko sees Abel pull up in late-model car.	Guliko: 'Were you there?' Abel: 'I wasn't well-received.' Guliko: 'Someone got in ahead of us.'		Abel went to new chief, presumably Tseretelo, for some kind of help; suggestion of plot.

Visual	Dialogue / Voice-over	Sound	Commentary
I 7 Night-time. Cemetery. Locked iron gate. **Ecu** of large padlock.			
Neighbor on balcony, bare-chested, takes deep chest-expanding breaths. Looks down to courtyard and sees Varlam sitting in garden chair, his legs outstretched.	Voice over: 'The lion's in a cage—let them try to get him now,' 'Pharaohs never had tombs like this.'	Crickets	Incongruity dominates, as the neighbor's complacency shatters at the sight of Varlam, and in Varlam's corpse's relaxed pose.
Cemetery, night; a line of motorcycle cops approaches grave. Tornike hides, rifle in hand. Officers are deployed, some with dogs, to catch the graverobber.		Shouts; so do relatives who come to look Vroom of bikes; footsteps; barks	
Abel sits, smokes, talks to friend, who takes him off to a nearby relative for supper; two sentries remain or guard.	Voice-over: 'No smoking or talking—be alert!'		
Cu of Tornike's watchful face.			
Sentry reads epitaph.	'That's enough [liquor], you'll croak.' 'Is this by Lucretius? What a poet!'	Gurgle of liquid Crickets	Sentries drink and chat: orders are not to be taken seriously, they simply go through the motions.
Figure in cap, holding shovel, approaches. Only Tornike notices. He aims as the person starts to dig. He fires.		Scraping	Only Tornike cares
Zoom in on the face of perpetrator.	Sentry: 'Halt or I'll fire! So you're the one who's been defiling our grave! You bastard! God, it's a woman!'	Shot; shouts, barks	Sentry shouts after Tornike has already fired.
Zoom in on Abel's face. In moonlight, woman holds hanky up to her face: it is Keti.			

3　Keti drags Varlam's corpse from its grave

Image	Sound	Dialogue	Commentary
I 8 Ls of red-carpeted central staircase. A woman in white flanked by two men emerges at top and begins to descend. The men wear medieval armor and carry halberds. Judge in wig and flat-topped velvet cap plays with Rubik's cube. Other judges and lawyers similarly attired. Keti wears white suit, black sling, lace-trimmed white hat. In first row of spectators, Guliko wears white fur stole, black dress, necklace.	Footsteps. Murmur of crowd below Band music.	Keti: 'I confirm [the exhumations] but do not admit my guilt.' Judge: 'You admitted your guilt at the inquest.' Keti: 'That's a lie. I never admitted my guilt... Judgment has been pronounced and the sentence passed. For as long as I'm alive, Varlam Aravidze will not lie in a grave. This sentence is final and not subject to appeal.'	Temporal disjunction. The incongruities of clothing, between words and facial expressions, and between judge's statements and Keti's, all testify to the inadequacy of the judicial and/or legal process to deal with moral issues.
Camera cuts from Keti's face, smiling slightly, to Guliko, to panel of judges. In foreground: defense counsel; in rear: Keti looking to one side, seemingly indifferent to lawyer. Head and shoulder shot of Keti, her head bent. She looks up at the judge's words and stands to make her statement. Keti takes the stand.		'My one wish is that this not be a settling of accounts with a dead man. I find no satisfaction in revenge. And so, who was Varlam Aravidze? I was eight years old when he became mayor of this city...'	The repeated shots of Guliko and Keti suggest that the two women embody opposing values.

4   The knights lead Keti to her trial

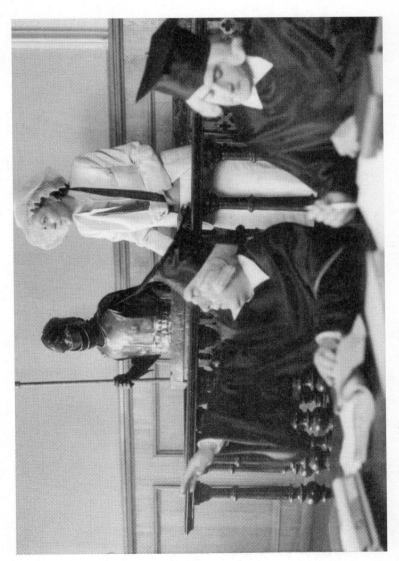

5   Keti proclaims her defiance

FLASHBACK

II 1 Girl blows bubbles on balcony, wearing white blouse and black vest; curtained window behind her, one red flower visible.

Kite flies nearly horizontally.

Overhead shot of stout women looking up and blowing kisses; parade.

Cut to head shot of Varlam, small-paned eye-glasses and tiny moustache, on balcony opposite; **Ls** of people gathered on balcony.

Features variously associated with Beria (glasses), Hitler (moustache), Mussolini (uniform).

High angle shot of worker in manhole fixing water pipe.

Cu of kite: figure is Varlam and a black falcon.

Cut to Keti, watching in delight.

Cut to burning effigy, wearing top hat.

Wall Street banker type, a common sight in Bolshevik parades of the Twenties.

Placard of Varlam; film cameraman in knickers perches on stairs.

Band music continues throughout scene.

Aural layering of water gushing, completely incomprehensible speeches.

Keti brings her mother out on to balcony.
Cut to street workers: water spouts.
Pan up bare legs of teenaged girl in red and white, making speech, while secretary, getting soaked, types record of speeches; workmen cover pipe with their bodies, to no avail.
Cut to Varlam, an associate standing behind him wearing identical moustache. Varlam emerges on to balcony, begins speaking. Sandro joins Keti and Nino; blocks Keti's pointing finger, leads them inside and closes the window.
Cut to Varlam, watching.

Click of window latch.

Slapstick.
Light reflected on window bounces off Varlam's glasses.

Varlam's associates find it polite to emulate him.

The men lock gazes.

Image	Sound	Commentary
II 2 Al fresco. Reverse zoom shows Nino, image of Christ, strange ridged cylindrical columns with no obvious function. A woman passes through, a rat on her headpiece and a long tail trailing. Fresco of Christ, hand upraised, disciple kneeling before him.	Male voice-over: 'Shortly before his death Einstein warned the world of a modern scientist's tragedy... Can it be that in his blind quest for scientific truths, he has forgotten his responsibility to mankind...?' Female voice-over: 'You have been listening to 'Great Minds of the World;' next, a program of dance music.'	Shot in sixth century church in Batumi. Image from Bosch painting; suggests a Georgian legend in which demons take possession of abandoned temples. Temporal disjunction: Einstein died in 1955. Profound moral dilemma of ends and means juxtaposed with banal popular culture.
Sandro stands near column; camera pans up to vaulted ceiling. Nino walks among columns, looks up at extensive scaffolding.	Scratchy record of early swing. English lyrics: 'There was little Jack Horner and Bo-peep too/The old woman who lived in a shoe,/As everyone knows, the question arose,/Who made Little Boy Blue?'	Lyrics suggest the co-optation of folklore for entertainment purposes.
Zoom in on fresco of Adam and Eve, expelled from Eden.	*A capella* chant.	Costs of quest for knowledge; portent of Sandro and Nino's fate.

6   Varlam, in the conservatory garden, listens to Sandro, Moise and Miriam

II 3 Varlam is seated amid greenery. He smiles as Sandro speaks.	Sandro asks for expedited construction of new research institute and an end to explosions. Otherwise 'the church will crumble.' Varlam: 'So you're opposed to science and progress?' Sandro: 'We're against any science that destroys cultural monuments.'		Sandro recognizes the need for research, but not at cost of cultural destruction. (Einstein said that science 'without religion is lame, religion without science is blind.')
Camera pulls back: Sandro is with older couple, by appearance well-to-do members of the *intelligentsia*. Doksopoulo enters, stands at center screen. Varlam is nearly off-screen.	Doksopoulo: 'It's a breeding ground for unsanitary conditions.... Nobody goes to your church anymore.' Sandro: 'Destroying it means severing the roots that nourish the people spiritually.' He compares it to Dante, Homer, Verdi, to Notre Dame and St Peter's. Varlam calls Moise and Miriam, the older couple, 'blue-bloods'; asks about	Birds twitter throughout.	It is not, as it seemed, a duel between Varlam and Sandro alone. Varlam uses others to speak for him. Sandro includes two specific Georgian names: Rustaveli and Svetntskhoveli, the latter a church.
Varlam seems convinced; he tears up his own order. Behind Sandro, rippling water of a pool.	Sandro's great-great-grandfather, claims they share an ancestor. Asks about girl who blew bubbles. 'I notice everything—so beware of me. Some blow bubbles, others track down enemies of the people. Murderers kill, beggars beg, sluts walk the streets...'		Their names suggest not aristocrats but Old Testament Jews, Moses and his sister Miriam.
Varlam's face changes, his smile disappears and reappears.		Abruptly; Khachaturian's 'Saber Dance'	

Suddenly his face contorts and he screams:

[in **Russian**] Is that normal? IS THAT NORMAL?'

Moise looks around, disconcerted

Cu of pendant fruit, doubling as a microphone.
Camera points straight up at palm fronds, glass roof of solarium; zoom to guards above, pacing on roof; they wear medieval armor and carry halberds.
Varlam looks up at black-leather-jacketed, bowler-hatted woman who approaches.
Cut to old-fashioned gramophone with horn.

She: 'The audience is over.'

This is the first reference to Stalin's well-known obsession with concealed enemies. In a letter he sent key Party organizers in 1936, he wrote, 'The inalienable quality of every Bolshevik ... should be the ability to recognize an enemy of the party, no matter how well he may be masked.'[1]

In the Twenties black leather jackets were worn by Cheka members.

II 4 Dimly-lit room, high ceiling. Sepia tones. Man—Mikhail Korisheli—sits behind desk. Sandro paces.			
	'Maybe Aravidze really doesn't know anything.' Sandro feels responsible for arrest of Moise and Miriam; Mikhail reassures him. 'I'll take up the question. Varlam will look into it and report to me.' (Into phone) 'We must be more careful in such matters, Varlam.'	Typing.	
Korisheli's wife, Elena, smokes.			
Korisheli is clean-cut, well-groomed, white-cuffed.			Clothing identifies him as a cultured *intelligent* and his confident power marks him as the epitome of an Old Bolshevik.
Hangs up, turns to Sandro; heavily reasonable tone of voice.		Phone rings.	
	To Sandro: 'Varlam looked into it and released them.'		
Elena smiles slightly.			Her faith is confirmed.

7   The Baratelis, *en famille*

8   Varlam at the Barateli flat, with Sandro

II 5 Keti in party dress runs to apartment door. Paintings cover the apartment walls. In doorway two men in tailcoats; Doksopoulo holds a birdcage, his associate a bouquet of red flowers. They part to reveal Varlam in a white sheepskin mantle. From under the mantle, a boy emerges.		Doorbell.	Shot in Tbilisi apartment-museum of Georgian artist, Elena Akhvlediani.
Cut to **cu** of Keti, warmly smiling; Nino, in red, warmly smiling.	Varlam introduces his son Abel. Varlam: 'I don't know whether Sandro resembles the great Sandro Boticelli, but Nino reminds me of Boticelli's divine Madonnas. ... We kiss the hands of mere mortals, but bow low to goddesses and saints.' He reassures Sandro that Moise and Miriam—'the old guard, eh?'—have been released.	Varlam sings, they echo.	Varlam's manner and speech are theatrical; he laughs often. The others hardly say a word. Keti and Nino are naive. Varlam presents himself as cultured and cultivated, with his reference to Botticelli; his singing, his recitation. He suggests that he and Sandro are on the same side.
Varlam falls to the floor, laughingly reassures her. Kisses the hem of her gown. Keti moves to her father's side, and he pulls her close; he does not smile.			
Varlam kisses Keti's hand, gives her the birdcage. **Ecu** of his large hand blocking her face behind the bars of the cage, an ominous image. Varlam, foregrounded, moves about the room, looks at paintings. Rack focus to Sandro and Nino behind Varlam. Nino smiles, Sandro does not. Elena joins them, nodding approvingly.	'This is the kind of art we need, serious, thoughtful art. But you'll have enemies, they'll say *Such art is intimate, boudoir art, an escape from reality.* I would answer that escape from one reality may mean entrance into another, greater reality. The people need a great reality, though enemies may see this as a call to anarchy...'	Varlam leads the two men in 'la-la'.	This criticism was levelled at Abuladze for his 1958 film, *Someone Else's Children.* Sandro is wary, Elena is a believer.

Varlam inspects a painting.

Sandro lowers his head, Elena pats his shoulder.

Cut to Doksopoulo, staring blankly; his associate, Riktafelov, primps in the mirror.

Varlam sits on steps as he speaks; a traditionally-woven black, white and red rug hangs behind him.

Varlam: 'I'd like to look into their brains. Ah, Sandro, at least these are literate... Artists like you must be with us now. We're charged with a great mission—to raise their cultural level.'

Sandro: 'Can I, through painting, or you, through your efforts, enlighten a people that created *The Knight in the Panther's Skin?* Only a spiritual leader, a moral hero, can enlighten the people.'

Cut to Sandro, staring at him.

Varlam replies [in Russian]: 'Modesty becomes a man.'

Camera stays on Varlam, who is smiling, as Sandro turns away. Light glints on Varlam's glasses; his eyes are invisible.

Notes:

Same clock as in Abel and Guliko's room.

Tinkly melody of clock, then chimes.

Georgia's national epic, by the twelfth-century poet Shota Rustaveli.

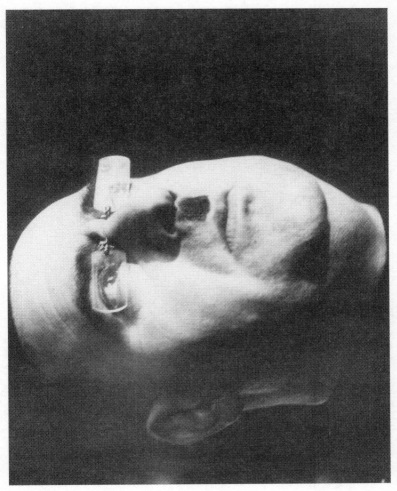

9   Varlam admires Sandro's paintings

II 6 Cut to crucifix, the two children.	Abel asks why Christ was tortured, and Keti replies, 'For the truth'. She tells him not to worry, that Christ—like all kind people—is in heaven.	Soft, rhythmic thumping, source unknown.	
Nino, in doorway, overhears. She puts down a basket of pears and kneels before Abel.	Abel asks, 'Can [the cross] make my mother alive again?' Nino: 'She loves you. She's in heaven with the angels now.'		Sincerity of her gesture heightens theatricality of Varlam's earlier pose.
Varlam in the foreground, his two cohorts behind. He gestures, they gesture.		Varlam sings Manrico's aria from *Il Trovatore*, the two men provide oom-pa; applause.	Beria loved to sing operatic arias.
Sandro, Nino and Eleni watch from the couch.			Repeating his gestures precisely, they have no minds of their own; they are entirely Varlam's creatures.
Cut to children at keyboard.	Keti asks if Abel may stay a bit longer and Varlam agrees. Elena asks Varlam for an encore; Sandro seconds the request. Varlam recites Shakespeare's Sonnet 66, omitting the last two lines.		
Sandro sits on the couch, arms around the two women; Doksopoulo and Riktafelov flank them.			
Abel kisses Keti, jumps out the window.	Varlam [in Russian]: 'Rules are rules. Allez-oop!'		See Chapter 3.
Nino clutches Sandro in dismay; Keti runs to window; Varlam, wearing white mantle, laughs and jumps. Elena is amazed and impressed.	Keti: 'Mama, he galloped away!' Sandro: 'The buffoon!'	Horse whinnies; clip-clop.	
Nino turns to open the door. Varlam apologizes for returning.	Varlam: 'My silly boy carried off your cross. Take care of it, it's valuable.'	Doorbell. Clock melody, chimes once.	What Guliko said when she hid Varlam's portrait: re-enforces link between them.

10   (L to R): Doksopoulo, Nino, Sandro, Elena Korisheli and Riktafelov, listen to Varlam recite Shakespeare

11   Varlam prepares to exit the Barateli flat, as young Keti watches

II 7 Sandro is hunched over the piano, Nino sleeps in a chair, wrapped in a shawl. She dreams: a man walks down a long dark corridor, his feet in water. Then two figures become visible at the end of corridor; they run. We realize they are Sandro and Nino: they run hand-in-hand through deserted streets. An armed and armored horseback rider blocks them at one end; a car follows from the other. Varlam rides in the car. They run up iron stairs, across a freshly-plowed field. Deep in rear, **els**, an ox pulls a plow. Both horseman and Varlam (in car) pursue Sandro and Nino. The city is visible far in the background.		Corridor resembles underground corridors of prisons such as the Lubianka.

He plays Debussy.

Water sloshing, louder as they run.
Click of door being locked. |
| Overhead shot: Nino and Sandro buried to their necks in earth. Peasant waves to Varlam and runs toward car. Zoom in on Varlam, cut to Sandro, whose eyes are open. Nino winces slightly. Cut to Varlam, singing and gesticulating; he laughs. Nino starts awake. She and Sandro cling to each other. | Nino: 'I had a terrible dream. Let's go to some far-off place.' Sandro replies that if 'they need to,' they'll get us from under the earth.' | Eerie noise, like wind-tunnel.

Abruptly: Italian *bel canto*.

Doorbell. |

Sandro opens door to two armored men; one we recognize as Doksopoulo. He goes to the piano, while Sandro dons a white shirt, tie, jacket, black hat, and is escorted out. Nino watches, tearful. One man carries out canvases.

Doksopoulo: 'Peace unto this house. Are you Sandro Barateli? Come with us. It won't be for long.'

He picks out a tune; hits discordant notes.

Arrests were often made in the middle of the night, and those arrested were often reassured that they would soon return home.

12   Abel sings an aria from his car, in Nino's dream

13 Nino and Sandro are buried alive, in Nino's dream

II 8 A large room, empty of furniture except for a piano and desk. Korisheli enters and sits at the desk, Varlam remains standing. Varlam shows papers; Korisheli reads aloud.	They discuss Sandro's arrest. Korisheli reads: '*The daubing of some pseudo-artist has taken on the features of individualism. This pompous artist is a hooligan... Who is shielding this lunatic?... If you do not investigate, we'll appeal to higher authorities. (Signed) A group of artists.*	Characteristic language of anonymous denunciations.
Korisheli wears a suit, his black hair is well-coiffed. He is outraged.	'You mean Barateli was arrested because of this filth? Those who wrote it are enemies of the nation. It's insanity. Barateli is my friend, my pupil.' Varlam: 'I understand you. By the way, he happens to be my relative. And a close one at that. I'm only fulfilling the holy will of the people... File a protest, I've nothing against that.' Korisheli: 'What could you have against the truth?... One intelligent person is worth a thousand idiots.' Varlam: 'Your friend and my relative is now our enemy.' Korisheli: '... Who is the enemy?'	Korisheli still thinks he is in control. He uses the informal form of address to Varlam (who uses the formal), though he becomes wary when he hears of Varlam's 'kinship' with Sandro.
Korisheli lowers his head on to his hands. Varlam smiles.		Varlam's hand was forced, he claims.
Korisheli stares at him, crumples the denunciation. His voice rises with his agitation, while Varlam remains calm and impassive.		Korisheli cannot believe his ears.
Cu of Varlam's face.		
Korisheli strikes him, his pince-nez falls.		Tinkle of breaking glass.

II 9 Sepia tones. Woman carries a child past a long line, approaches opening. She hands in a chit. She sobs with joy, hugs the child. Older woman hands in chit, gives name.	She repeats that women with children don't have to wait in line. 'Your parcel was accepted.'	Music: scratchy recording of theme from *Sous les toits de Paris*.	
	'Exiled without right to correspond.'		During the Great Terror, this was a code phrase for 'executed'.
She shouts with anger and despair.	'Exiled to where? Why don't you just say that he's dead?'		
Nino and Keti approach window, give name.	'Exiled without right to correspond.'		
II 10 Cut to woman in black and white; drooping red flowers in vase. Nino enters hurriedly. Posters of Varlam lean against the wall. Nino grabs one and stomps on it. Slow pan to reveal Varlam in doorway. She sinks to her knees, kisses his shoes. Varlam stands stock-still, then steps over her.	Secretary tells Nino that Mikhail Korisheli was just arrested. 'Go away before you get into trouble.'	Birds twitter throughout.	
	'Mr Varlam help us, I beg of you. Sandro is perishing. Save him.'		Terrible inversion of Varlam's genuflection to her.

II 11 Young boy looks through the bars of a window into a cellar room. Nino and Keti run across a muddy railroad yard. Overhead shot of train-tops, piles of logs, watery mud. They scan cut ends of logs. Letters are visible on one log; a boy runs off shouting. Nino and Keti shown against browns of mud, logs, water. A forklift carries logs to enormous pile. Keti watches, runs back to check the cut ends; she is dwarfed by horizontals of logs and planks. A dog approaches and barks menacingly, but we hear nothing. Slow zoom along length of logs to Keti's face as she reads each one. Nino rests her face on her hands; Keti trails her fingers through sawdust. A cataract of sawdust. **Cu** of Keti watching, as a woman traces letters on logs with her fingertips. Her lips move, she kisses the surface and caresses the log. Vertical pan of Nino sitting on logs, Keti on her lap.	'Logs were unloaded at the railroad station, Aunty Nino. The names and addresses of exiles are on some of them.' 'Amiran Abashidze! I found him, mama!'	After Sandro's arrest Nino and Keti have had to move out of their spacious flat into a cellar. Originally this scene had dialogue, but when Abuladze filmed it, on location in Batumi, they taped the natural sounds and discarded the dialogue originally planned.[2]
	Mournful music.	
		Stalin was fond of the proverb, 'When you chop down a forest, chips fly.'
		Nino is defeated.

14 Woman strokes log carved by prisoner

II 12 Hard cut to white piano in leafy grove. A couple are seated on a bench. The groom wears a crown with a cross above his forehead; the bride wears an elaborate decorated headpiece. Sandro, bare-chested beneath a ripped shirt, stands against a stone wall. Bride, blindfolded, holds scale in one hand, knife in the other.	The 'groom' *cum* interrogator tells Sandro that 'a sincere confession' will mitigate his case; that Korisheli has implicated him. Sandro refuses to believe him: 'If men like Korisheli are being arrested, you may as well arrest the whole country.'	Mendelssohn's *Wedding March*. Man hums, abruptly stops. Birds twitter throughout.	Traditional Georgian wedding finery. After the excruciating realism of the preceding scenes, and their dim lighting, the hard sunlight and the bizarre costuming and setting are quite jarring.
Camera cuts back and forth between Sandro and his interrogator. **Ms** of blind justice. **Ls** of Korisheli, wearing a long white hospital-type gown. Armed men follow him. Interrogator hops onto the piano, stretches out. Korisheli's black hair is grey and dishevelled, his chin covered with white stubble. Sandro watches in horror. At each of Korisheli's responses, the interrogator motions to Sandro: *you see?*	Korisheli confesses to having been a spy; his assignment, he says, was to dig a tunnel from Bombay to London. When asked how many were involved, he says, '2700 men. There's a list.' He numbers among their crimes planting 'poisoned corn'. He agrees that Sandro was a member of his 'gang'.	Sounds of hot summer day, amplified.	Similarly absurd charges and admissions abound in the records of the arrests and interrogations of the Thirties.

15   The 'groom' *cum* interrogator with his 'bride'

Interrogator escorts Justice out of grove. Korisheli places his palms flat on the piano, lowers his ear to the soundboard, breaks off a branch, and carefully places it under piano lid.	Korisheli reveals his strategy, to 'accuse as many people as possible. They can't arrest all of them. We'll sign any nonsense, finally the government will realize what's going on and will expose the malefactors...'		Though his tone of voice is 'reasonable,' his acts bespeak madness.
Sandro's eyes fill with tears.			
Korisheli notices. Korisheli raises his hands, then bangs his head down on the piano and falls to the ground.		He whimpers, then howls.	Momentarily he seems sane. Lear-like.
		Discordant twang.	

16 Mikhail Korisheli confesses

II 13 Ls of balcony with microphone. Varlam emerges. On the left, a gallows with a vulture or crow perched on the crosspiece. **Ecu** of Varlam, who modulates his voice from a shout to a whisper, his expression from a grimace to a smile.	'We must be vigilant and ready to unmask any foe ... Four out of three persons are enemies ... Our motherland is in danger ... It's difficult to catch a black cat in a dark room, especially if there's no cat there. But we will.'	Band music, same as on the day of Varlam's inauguration.	The clichés of Stalinism include 'vigilance', unmasking of enemies, the danger to the motherland...
II 14 Elena enters an office, smiling, carrying flowers and globe. Nino stands at the window. Elena phones Varlam's secretary. She hangs up, and turns to Nino, who remains silent and still.	Elena welcomes her. She asks the secretary if there's any news of our men'. Reassures Nino that 'all will be well'; that the arrests of Sandro and Mikhail were a mistake. 'We must be patient, both of us. They'll investigate and release them ... We're serving a great cause. Some innocent people may suffer. But I can already hear Beethoven's *Ode to Joy*, it will resound throughout the world.'	Band music audible in the background.	
Nino looks away. Elena's face is exalted: Nino's impassive.		She sings a verse, in German; chorus and orchestra continue the final movement throughout this scene.	

17   The knights watch Sandro's sentencing

Sepia tones. Sandro, in a white shirt and black vest, walks along a corridor, a single light shining behind him. He is reflected in muddy water beneath him. A figure entirely hidden in armor reads from a paper. **Cu** of Sandro listening, his lips moving as if in prayer. **Cu** of typewriter, cuffs, fingers typing. Sandro ascends stairs; Blind Justice is visible behind him. Varlam's secretary watches. Sandro's body is reflected in water: vertical pan up his bare legs, white cloth wrapped around his loins, to hands cuffed above his head. He hangs beneath bare lights, his face contorted in pain; focus blurs. Nino sits up abruptly.		The charges; the 'protocol'.
		Sandro looks very Christ-like, and the scene is—though without crosspiece—one of a crucifixion.
Nino pushes her way through a crowd.	She tells an anxious Keti, 'We've lost our papa.' Voice: 'They've blown up the church after all.'	A single shot, then explosions.

18   Sandro prepares for his execution

II 16 Through an open archway. Nino runs forward and up stairs. Rings bell, bangs on door.	Woman's voice: 'There's nobody there. Elena's been arrested.'	Hurried footsteps.	
Nino slowly descends, sits on step, weeps.		Mournful strings.	Her isolation is total. Reprise of melody heard in log scene at railroad yard.
II 17 Doksopoulo opens the office door. Varlam is on the phone. Doksopoulo smiles, pleased with himself.	Doksopoulo: 'I've brought them in, Mr Varlam. The Darbaiselis. As you said. They're down there, in the truck.'		The name was originally Amilakhvari, an ancient family with not one survivor, but Abuladze changed the name: he felt that Georgian audiences would find the reference too painful.[3]

19 Doksopoulo informs Varlam of his arrest of the Darbaiselis

Varlam walks to window. From his viewpoint we see a truck in the courtyard below, with perhaps 50 people, and three guards in armor.	Varlam: 'Send them all home immediately.' Doksopoulo: 'I thought you'd be glad to see I rounded up a truckful of enemies. All Riktafelov did was track down one spy, and he got a five-room flat and a commendation. You mean all my work was for nothing?' Varlam tells him to send them home and write a letter of resignation, to which Doksopoulo replies, 'But you know I'm illiterate.' Varlam: 'Get out!'	An allusion to the venal motives that prompted many of those active in the security apparatus.
Doksopoulo smiles beseechingly.		
Varlam shouts. Doksopoulo listens outside door as Varlam talks to secretary; her hand rests on his shoulder as she whispers. When Doksopoulo re-enters, Varlam smiles benevolently.	Varlam: 'All right, to hell with them and you. We'll jail them all.' Doksopoulo thanks him profusely.	Having disposed of the *intelligentsia*, Varlam is left with the ignorant and uneducated.
After Doksopoulo leaves, Varlam removes his glasses and rubs his eyes.		

II 18 Dimly-lit cellar.

Nino wraps Keti in a shawl. As they move toward the door, the shadow of a halberd is seen, followed by two men.

Varlam's secretary warns Nino of her impending arrest, gives her tickets and money.
Nino: 'We must hurry, to the village.'
Man's voice: 'Peace unto this house. Are you Nino Barateli?'

Some people did manage to avoid arrest by fleeing to out-of-the-way places.

A horse-drawn wagon drives down the street. Nino is shoved into the back, behind a barred door. Light picks out her hands reaching out through the bars, Keti's reaching up to her.

Clip-clop.

Keti: 'Mama! Mama!'
Nino: 'Don't be frightened, Keti!'

III 1 Courtroom. **Cu** of Keti. Reverse zoom. Guliko looks back over her bare shoulder at Tornike, seated some rows back.	Keti: 'That was the end of Nino Barateli. On my behalf, and on behalf of all the innocent victims, I demand that Varlam Aravidze be exhumed by his kin.'	Keti's account of Varlam's guilt is news only to Tornike.
Pan to Abel, who rises from his chair.	Abel protests: 'Everything she said was a pack of lies.' Others echo him.	
Judge gavels for order. Spectator who curses Keti is removed from the courtroom. One of the assessors plays with a Rubik's cube.	Guliko: 'Aren't we to bury the deceased?' Keti: 'No! To bury him means to forgive him!'	

III 2 **Cu** of Tornike, in profile. Slow zoom in on white-walled enclosure. Sunlight streams through vertical gaps. A white-clad figure pushes back black hood: Varlam. Tornike gazes at him: he is white-haired and grizzled. Fast zoom in on Varlam, who shouts and runs toward the wall, holds up an imaginary gun and fires. He starts to strut around enclosure, laughing and squinting at the sun.

Varlam lies down on black cloth, covers his forehead. **Ecu** of Tornike, who turns and shouts, running from one side of enclosure to another.

Varlam: 'No one is sinless, my boy. We were all born in sin. Help me, Tornike! The sun is rising. Why is that ray after me? Let's block it out, or I'll bleed to death.... Look at my fingers—see the blood dripping. (*To sunray*) Why are you after me? Why are you searching out my soul? I'll put you out, I'll destroy you. Beh... Beh... There, it's gone out.'

Tornike: 'Grandpa's dead! Mama, mama! Grandpa's dead!'

Birds twitter throughout.

The birdsong links this scene with the others in which birds twittered: the exhumation, the interrogation.

Linkage between Varlam's earlier recital of Shakespeare sonnet and Shakespeare's guilt-ridden tragic figures: the light imagery recalls *Othello*, the blood *Macbeth*.

20 Tornike daydreams about Grandpa Varlam

III 3 Roomful of people, Abel in the foreground.	One guest jokes that since people say his father is a 'bad man', he'll have to exhume his father's corpse too.		
Abel enters the empty courtroom, sees Tornike. Camera cuts back and forth between Abel and Tornike; Abel moves to windows, to judges' chairs.	Tornike challenges him: 'Did you know all of that?' Abel: 'Your grandfather never did wrong. Those were complicated times. It's difficult to explain now.' Tornike rejects the argument: 'What do the times have to do with it?' Abel: 'A lot. It was a question of to be or not to be. We were surrounded by foes.' Sandro, he says, was one of them, a good artist, but 'he didn't understand a lot…. We made mistakes—but what are the lives of one or two people compared to the well-being of millions?'	Burst of laughter.	Manipulation of Shakespearean profundities for trivial or self-serving purposes.
Cu of Tornike.	Tornike: 'You justify Grandpa and follow in his footsteps. You've no pity for that woman. You should ask her to forgive you.'		
Abel faces camera, Tornike behind him. As Abel rants, Tornike starts walking out of courtroom.	Abel: 'Are you crazy?' Tornike: 'I hate you! Hate you!'		

21 Tornike in shock in the courtroom after Keti's tale

III 4 Tornike lies immobile on his bed. Abel stands outside the door, Guliko and a doctor are at the bed. On the wall hang a rifle and a poster of a bullfighter.	Doctor reassures Guliko: 'Tornike is at a "vulnerable" age, shocked by the daily sight of a corpse, but he'll recover'.	
Tornike's vision: Guliko, in black dress and heels, dances around Varlam's corpse in the courtyard of their house. The corpse raises its head, dons his spectacles, smiles with satisfaction, turns as if to sleep. **Cu** of poster: bullfighter stands over stricken animal.	Drums; electric guitar	Even more than Abel, Guliko is Varlam's natural heir; he can sleep, knowing she is in charge and will continue his legacy.

III 5 Tableful of men. Guliko stands behind Abel, who is preoccupied; he mostly listens and doesn't say much. A gangster type, wearing a black shirt open at the throat, makes a suggestion.

They discuss what will happen to Keti. Guliko complains that if she sees Varlam's corpse once more, she'll go mad. Gangster: 'I'll send my boys to see her. They'll whisper a few words, and she'll shut up.' Guliko: 'There must be limits. It's time for action.' Abel: 'Can't you see, I'm losing my son.' Guliko: 'Don't hide behind my son. My boy is no coward.'

Guliko is the more powerful, though she outwardly defers to Abel: Lady Macbeth, untroubled by conscience.

III 6 Courtroom. One lawyer jumps up theatrically. He reads, holding his glasses up to his eyes with the lenses inverted. Keti sits behind him, watching Guliko, who smiles.

Lawyer: 'The trial must be stopped. (*He reads from report*) *The defendant is not mentally ill. She is psychopathic, given to emotional acts.* The law forbids us to try the mentally ill.'

Keti's defense attorney jumps up no less theatrically.

Defense: 'Such arrogant and frivolous judgments are sacrilegious. An awful spiritual wound and horrible living conditions were harmful to her health and warped her character. But the defendant's act was not premeditated, it was a fit of passion, a protest.'

The lawyers' arguments make no sense. Everyone truly involved—Keti, Abel, Guliko—knows that the legal debate is completely immaterial and irrelevant to the outcome.

Cu of Abel. His vision: an overhead shot of the white-walled enclosure, ringed by empty chairs. In the center, banks of red flowers. Pall-bearers carry a coffin, wave to empty seats.
Cut to Tornike on his bed.

Sussuration.

Clock melody.

Like a bull-fighter waving triumphantly to his fans.

III 7 Abel lights a candle, descends stairs. He holds the light up to a crucifix on wall. Light picks out two hands, stripping flesh off fish. Camera remains on Abel, his hand holding the candle.

Cut to a pan along stacks of paintings and icons stacked against the wall. An image of two faces—both Abel—refracted in mirrors.
Cu of ravening mouth gorging on fish.
Doubled image of Abel.
Cu of fish skeleton.

Abel: 'Lord.'
Voice: 'What is it, my son.'
Abel: 'My soul is split in two. I preach atheism but I wear a cross. I'm losing my moral principles, I can no longer distinguish good from evil, I can justify any baseness...'
Voice, through a mouth full of food: 'Who are you deceiving, you hypocrite? You will pulverize anyone who stands in your way. It's not a split personality that bothers you, it's fear. You always gloated about your model family. Now it's all crumbling. You will be alone, weak, helpless ... terrified of the prospect of loneliness.'
Abel protests, but then yields: 'Yes, I am afraid. I feel I'm in a void. I pretend, I lie. Who am I? What is the purpose of my life? Who are you, Abel Aravidze? Abel Aravidze? Abel Aravidze?'
The voice chides him: 'Forget all this nonsense. You're just a coward.'
Abel: 'Who are you? Tell me who are you!'

Abuladze: 'I consider Abel even more dangerous than Varlam ... because, with his split consciousness, his behavior is unpredictable... People like Abel are the spawning grounds for future Varlams.'[4]

Varlam, one lens glinting light. Zoom: he brays a laugh.

Varlam: 'Don't you recognize me, son? Why do you come to the devil to confess your sins?'

Glass breaks.

III 8 Courtroom. Guliko wears a sequinned top, white stole.
Abel holds the fish skeleton. Guliko feeds him pills.

Abel: 'I've no strength left. My life is over.'
Guliko: 'Get a grip. Everyone is looking at us.'
Keti reiterates her determination to exhume Varlam 'the minute I'm released.' The procurator counters: 'I wouldn't like to think that Mme Barateli believes one can achieve a moral good through immoral behavior.'
Keti is defiant: 'I can, for Aravidze is not dead! As long as you defend him, he lives on and corrupts society.'
The procurator takes her belief that Varlam 'is alive' as evidence of her mental illness.

Keti waves and turns to leave.

Keti: 'Goodbye, honorable members of the court, honorable ladies and gentlemen. I'll exhume him anyway.'

Keti sees through the procurator's spurious 'morality'.
In 1969 General Piotr Grigorenko, an active participant in the human rights movement, was examined by a psychiatrist at the Serbsky Institute. She asked him what motivated his 'anti-state' activities. 'I could not breathe,' he replied. 'You should have seen how her eyes flashed with joy, how quickly she jotted down my reply in her notebook. . .proof that a maniac sat before her.'[5]

III 9 Keti sits at a barred window, lighting a cigarette. She recites a poem.

Door opens: Tornike enters. Rack focus between Keti in foreground, Tornike in rear.

Each face is framed in a square formed by bars of window grate.

Keti: 'Evening. Spring. Rollcall of shadows. A bird jumps from branch to branch. I want to give myself up to a new dream. The moon is weary of admiring the earth.' He asks her forgiveness. She replies, 'I'm not God, to give you absolution.' He reminds her that he fired at her and calls himself a murderer. Keti: 'What an ill-fated star I was born under. I even turned you, poor innocent, into a murderer. I'm mad, I really am. Tomorrow they'll cart me off to an insane asylum.' Tornike: 'An insane asylum?'

She is pensive, weary.

Tornike, unaware of his parents' scheme, is horrified.

22 Keti in jail

23   Tornike visits Keti in jail

III 10 **Cu** of hands. Slow pan to music score, candelabra, vase. Men stand near the piano, listening to Abel play. Guliko watches, smoking. Abel takes Tornike by the hand, leads him out of the room. Guliko follows.		Opening bars of *Moonlight Sonata*. In background arpeggio.	
	Tornike's voice: 'What have you done, Mama?'		Tornike intuitively understands that his mother is responsible for Keti's sentence.
Father and son argue; Guliko tries in vain to intervene.	Abel: 'What are you accusing me of? The court decided she's insane.' Tornike: 'She's not insane and she's not guilty. How can you go on lying forever? All you care about is your own well-being; doesn't your conscience bother you? It bothered Grandpa, that's why he hid in the bunker. I hate you all. This is no house, it's a tomb. How can you call yourself a man?'		
Abel slaps Tornike and leaves. As guests arrive, bearing bottles and gifts, Tornike runs to his room and locks himself in. Guliko, outside, is frantic. Tornike's leg, sprawled. Abel cracks the door open, looks in, closes it. **Cu** of rifle barrel, inscribed, *To my beloved grandson from Grandpa Varlam.*		Ragtime music audible *Sunny.*	
	Guliko calls out: 'Abel!'	A shot.	
Abel in darkness; a few rays of light seem to show he is in an empty courtroom.	He curses himself, his life, his deeds. 'What have you done, you monster. Abel Aravidze? Why were you born, you fiend, Abel Aravidze? And your father and your son, why were they born?'		
Hard cut to Abel, deep in hole he has dug. His shirt is sodden. At the precipice, with skyscrapers of modern city visible in background, he drags body by its heels and (**els**) hurls it over hillside.		Train chugs; bird calls.	He's been digging all night.

III 11 Upside-down photo of Varlam in the paper. Keti reads the obituary aloud, while a hand holding a fork scrapes up cake from a plate. Pan up to Keti's face.	*'A true son of his homeland, a model citizen and an irreproachable man has passed away...'*	Guitar music.	Abuladze: 'Keti's icing churches have no connection to what is genuine, they are *ersatz*, people eat up the sugar-temple without a thought.'[16]
Keti, at the fridge, takes out eggs. The table is covered with cakes, mostly frosted with churches.	Keti: 'So you knew Aravidze well?' Man's voice: 'He was a good man, a great man.' Keti: 'I hear his sins gave him no peace.' Man's voice: 'Don't be silly. His one concern was to be of help to people.'		
An old lady in black and white, with a red flower in her bedraggled hat, approaches the window. She carries a suitcase in one hand.	Old woman: 'Is this the road to the church?' Keti: 'This is Varlam Street. It doesn't lead to a church.' Old woman: 'Then what good is it, if it doesn't lead to a church?'	Tap at window.	
Camera follows her as she walks up the street, away from house; from the window Keti watches her recede into the distance.		Choral music.	

Notes

1 Cited by Ronald Grigor Suny, *The Making of the Georgian Nation*, 2nd edn (Bloomington, Ind.: Ind, Univ. Press, 1994), p. 274.
2 *Nigde i vezde. Nikogda i vsegda.* ['Nowhere and Everywhere. Never and Always'] (Abuladze interview with Neya Zorkaya), *Novoe vremia*, 6 February 1987, in Viktor Bozhovich (ed.) *Pokaianie* (Moscow: 1988), p. 12.
3 *O proshlom dlia budushchego.* ['About the Past for the Sake of the Future'] (Abuladze interview with Lidya Pol'skaya), *Literaturnaia gazeta*, 25 February 1987, in Bozhovich, p. 16.
4 *O proshlom dlia budushchego.* ['About the Past for the Sake of the Future'] (Abuladze interview with Lidya Pol'skaya), *Literaturnaia gazeta*, 25 February 1987, in Bozhovich, p. 16.
5 Pyotr Grigorenko, *The Grigorenko Papers*, (Boulder, Co.: Westview Press, 1973), pp. 142–3.
6 *O proshlom dlia budushchego.* ['About the Past for the Sake of the Future'] (Abuladze interview with Lidya Pol'skaya), *Literaturnaia gazeta*, 25 February 1987, in Bozhovich, p. 16.

3. Signs and Symbols:
Repentance's Stylistic Devices

Abuladze's repertory of stylistic devices is varied and impressive. As Tatiana Khloplyankina noted, *Repentance* 'speaks to us in the language of metaphors and symbols'.[1] These stylistic devices include numerous visual anachronisms, fantasy and reverie, music, literary and historical allusion, in addition to the imaginative use of color, cutting, camera movement and the extreme close-up. The most consistent, most obvious, and perhaps most important device contributing to the picture's overriding surrealism appears early in the film—anachronism.

Anachronism

Movie anachronisms typically situate items from the present in the past, as the famous example from the Twenties, of Rudolph Valentino's wristwatch-sporting Sheikh, demonstrates. Abuladze, however, prefers what we might dub a 'counteranachronism': the placement of details from the past into the present. These details undercut the viewer's efforts to establish the timeframe from the *mise-en-scène* and therefore serve as universalizing signs in the cinematic text. In the opening scene, the baker (Keti) and her guest are dressed in more or less modern (if not obviously contemporary) clothing, yet Keti's customer comes by the window in the evening clothes of a more formal era, riding in a horse-drawn carriage, perhaps a re-enactment of traditional wedding rites. Likewise, when Varlam is unearthed for a second time, the police haul him away in an obviously outdated vehicle that looks suspiciously reminiscent of the 'paddy wagon' or Black Maria that carried victims of the Terror away during the Stalin era.

More important examples of this self-conscious placement of details from the past into the present can be found in the continued use of costumes recalling the late Middle Ages or Renaissance, especially various types of armor. This device, though it has been disparaged as 'more than simple',[2] in fact provides one visual link between the officialdom in the second framing story's courtroom scenes and those surrounding Varlam Aravidze in the flashback. (Another is color, to be discussed below.) Although no particular time period is overtly established for the second framing story, the way the Aravidzes and their friends are dressed for the funeral indicates a more or less contemporary timeframe. Likewise, the white suit Keti wears for her courtroom appearance, although absurdly glamorous for the occasion, is of a reasonably modern cut. But the guards who escort her into the courtroom are arrayed in full armor, and the panel of comic-opera judges, lawyers and court officials are dressed in faux-Elizabethan garb. (In an especially ironic visual pun, the bewigged head judge plays unsuccessfully with a Rubik's cube throughout the proceedings. In this particular instance, which is the anachronism?) The overall effect is nonetheless obvious: this 'trial' is an Inquisition.

The flashback appears to be set in the Thirties, an assessment again based primarily on costuming, particularly on Varlam's frameless eyeglasses (recalling those worn by Lavrenti Beria) and his Hitler/Mussolini-style uniform. But here as well, the cohort of guards and Varlam's enforcers wear full armor. We first see this when Varlam meets with Sandro, Moise and Miriam in the greenhouse garden; while they talk, the camera cuts away to the glass roof of the greenhouse. Armored knights are walking overhead, occasionally peering through the glass. These 'knights-in-shining-armor' eventually come to arrest Sandro, and, decades later, Keti. The agents of the Inquisition also utter anachronistic incantations—'Peace unto this house'—at the very moment when peace will be no more.

There are fewer examples of the more typical kind of anachronism in *Repentance*. One of these is, however, both eerie and memorable. In the garden sequence just mentioned, as Varlam listens, with an expression of sympathy and understanding, to the trio's arguments in favor of saving the church as a symbol of history and civilization, the fruit-laden trees begin to look more and more sinister. The pendulous fruits are in fact listening devices, recording every word these aristocratic and superfluous Judeo-Christian humanists utter against science and progress.

Fantasy and Reverie

Also critically important in shaping *Repentance* as an exercise in surrealism is Abuladze's frequent employment of fantasy/dream/daydream sequences throughout the course of the movie. These appear in both framing stories as well as in the flashback. Most obviously, the final scene of the film suggests that the *entire* film was, more than likely, nothing more than Keti's reverie as she decorated her cakes. But there are other important fantasies to consider, especially in the second half of the film.

The first of these occurs in the flashback, just after the unwelcome night visitors have left the Barateli apartment. As Sandro plays a mournful tune on the piano, Nino dozes. She dreams a fateful dream, about what in fact will soon befall them. In her dream, she and Sandro are vainly attempting to flee pursuers first unseen, then revealed as a demonic Varlam (in an open roadster) accompanied by his knights on horseback. Nino and Sandro run through sewers, through city streets, then out of town, until finally they are in the foothills high above Tbilisi. In a nod to another great surrealist film, Dali's *Un Chien Andalou*, Abuladze next shows us Nino and Sandro buried up to their necks in a newly plowed field. (There is a similar scene in Eisenstein's *Que viva Mexico!* as well).[3] Varlam, standing in his car, cheerfully belts out an aria from *Il Trovatore* (another Italian allusion) to his captive audience. Upon awaking, Nino tries to persuade her husband to run away, but Sandro ruefully responds that they will be 'tracked to the ends of the earth'. His arrest immediately follows; this is dream as prophesy.

Nino's second dream is also visionary. After Sandro's arrest, as Nino becomes more and more desperate, gradually emptying their apartment of its furnishings to support her futile struggle to save herself and her daughter, she dreams that Sandro is walking along a prison corridor on his way to his crucifixion. Nino is awakened from this nightmare by the sound of explosions: the historic church, symbol of the town's long and proud history and culture, has been destroyed (a pointed historical reference to the demolition by Stalin of the Cathedral Church of Christ the Savior in Moscow in 1931). Sandro, she knows instinctively, is dead.

The third important sequence in the flashback to consider as an exercise in surrealism is not a dream *per se*, but a fantasy representing the interrogation and torture of Sandro and Mikhail Korisheli. This fantasy is all the more vivid because it follows a long, intensely realistic and painful series of scenes showing Nino and Keti after Sandro's arrest. Abuladze juxtaposed the two quite consciously. As he explained in an interview with Lidya Pol'skaya that appeared in *Literaturnaia gazeta*:

> The entire image-system of the film permits multiple readings. But there are individual episodes that cannot sustain multiple interpretations. All viewers must understand them the same way ... We deliberately created these shifts from polysemantic to monosemantic, from ambiguity to simplicity.[4]

The episode begins with a scene that recalls Anna Akhmatova's famous poem *Requiem*. Nino waits in a long line outside the prison, with other hopeless women, trying to learn where Sandro is and whether she can send him a package. She is curtly informed, by a faceless official behind an impenetrable window, that Sandro has been 'exiled without the right to correspond'. Next, Nino attempts to make a personal appeal to Varlam, degrading herself with a touching and futile appeal to her helplessness, her beauty and indeed her sexuality (to which Varlam has obviously previously been attracted). Finally, and most brutally, Nino and Keti learn that logs cut by prisoner labor have arrived at a local lumber yard. They have been told that sometimes prisoners carve their names on them. Mother and daughter move from log to log, ankle deep in mud, but their desperate search yields no result. And when the lumber goes to the saw mill, all traces of their loved ones will vanish, reduced to dust.

After these three dreadful scenes, the return to surrealism is a jolt, but not unwelcome. A realistic depiction of Sandro's interrogation would be unendurable. So we find ourselves in a sunny and pleasant, if somewhat overgrown, garden. A couple in evening dress are seated together at a white grand piano playing Mendelssohn's *Wedding March*. Sandro, looking worn and dishevelled, his shirt bloodied and torn, suddenly appears to disturb this pretty scene. The jolly youngish gentleman at the piano turns out to be Sandro's inquisitor; his female partner stands to reveal herself as Blind Justice. The inquisitor blithely informs Sandro that his friend Mikhail Korisheli has implicated him in a vast political conspiracy. (It was not uncommon for the charges to be discovered *after* arrest in these extraordinary times.) Sandro is incredu-lous; he naively informs his persecutor that 'if men like [Korisheli] are being arrested, you might as well arrest the whole country.'

Korisheli is then brought in to corroborate the cheerful inquisitor's allegations. Korisheli is in very bad shape, both physically and mentally. His confession staggers Sandro: Korisheli admits to leading a conspiracy of 2700 men to 'dig a tunnel from Bombay to London' and to 'poison corn to annihilate the entire population'. Lips trembling, Korisheli explains to the stunned Sandro that he did, indeed, implicate Sandro and others: 'We must accuse as many people as possible and call them enemies of the people ... We'll sign everything and reduce it all to complete absurdity ... We'll sign a thousand stupid statements.' Korisheli breaks down, howling in anguish. Sandro's eyes glisten with tears.

As the film returns to the 'present', that is, the courtroom where Keti's trial is being held, the use of fantastical reveries as surrealist counterpoint to what passes for 'reality' continues. Tornike has two important daydreams. The first, which we have already discussed briefly, occurs just as Keti finishes her testimony about Varlam. Tornike, in his mind's eye, now sees his grandfather's soul laid bare. Varlam is a crazed and unkempt old man, imprisoned in a decaying castle (reminiscent of the many decaying castles hidden in Georgia's towering mountains), who fears the light of day as much as he fears the truth.

Tornike's second daydream, mentioned earlier, occurs when the Aravidzes return home after the trial's adjournment. As the scheming Guliko takes charge of the family's plot to put Keti away forever, Tornike is forced to realize that his mother is no more the person he wants her to be than was Varlam. In Tornike's fantasy, Guliko rejoices at Varlam's death, perhaps because it allowed *her* to assume the position of authority in the family and within their clique. By dancing around Varlam's corpse in the dream, Guliko might as well be dancing on his grave.

Music

The film's imaginative use of existing musical scores, selected by the film's screenwriter Nana Djanelidze, reinforces the surrealism of *Repen-tance* as well as underscoring intertextual motifs. The first instance of this device occurs at Varlam's funeral, when the mourners break into song. The tune is *Samshoblo*, which is not a funeral song, but rather a Georgian political anthem from the days of the short-lived Georgian Menshevik republic (1918–21).[5] *Samshoblo* therefore embodies Georgian independence, nationalism and opposition not to communism, but to Bolshevik (Soviet) power.

The next incidence of music employed as ironic counterpoint in the film is heard when Sandro visits the church *cum* laboratory to see for himself the damage the vibration testing has wrought. A radio is playing, and the music is definitely secular. We hear a doomsday speech by Einstein, immediately followed by *What Made Little Boy Blue?*, one of those jolly ditties that people in the Thirties found so uplifting, whether they were suffering from the ravages of the Great Depression, fascism or Stalinism.

Other musical interludes also provide pointed intertextual references. Shortly before his arrest, Sandro plays Debussy's haunting and impressionistic *Les Pas sur la neige*, which was also an important musical motif in the 1976 Soviet film *The Ascent* [*Voskhozhdenie*], Larissa Shepitko's harrowing cinematic tale of Soviet collaboration and betrayal during World War II.

Yet another musical reference alluding to the fascist era can be found after Mikhail Korisheli's arrest. Nino tries to get her friend Elena Korisheli, a true believer like Mikhail, to understand the implications of the terror that surrounds them. Elena believes that, regardless of the fates of their husbands, the 'great cause' they serve makes their sacrifices worthwhile. Face alight, she triumphantly begins to sing the Schiller *Ode to Joy* from Beethoven's Ninth ('Choral') Symphony, joined by a swelling chorus. (This music, which—like Wagner's—enjoyed special popularity during the Nazi era, serves as the segué to Nino's dream about Sandro's crucifixion.)

Finally, Varlam's fondness for Italian music, as exhibited in his visit to the Baratelis and in Nino's dream of their flight and live burial, is worth noting. Varlam, garbed like Mussolini, belting out an aria while Nino and Sandro are up to their necks in dirt, certainly makes one of the movie's more obvious points about the links between Stalinism and fascism.

There are also two noteworthy musical interludes in the final scenes of *Repentance*. When Tornike confronts his father for the last time, Abel is seated at the piano playing Beethoven's *Moonlight Sonata*. This piece, which links Abel to the founder of the Soviet state, was well-known to Soviet audiences as Lenin's favorite piece of music and has been used in other important Soviet films, like the 1934 classic *Chapayev*. And Tornike dies to the brash strains of the Seventies' American pop music hit *Sunny*, as his parents' crass friends, as insensitive to Georgian culture as their predecessors, bob up and down in a parody of Western dance.

Literary and Linguistic Quotation

Abuladze's literary and linguistic allusions are effectively marshalled to provide intertextual linkages. We have already mentioned that the scene of Nino and the other wives of the vanished standing in line recalls Akhmatova's *Requiem*, written in 1935–40, but unpublished until 1957 when it appeared abroad. The entire poem evokes the anguish Abuladze has rendered in images in *Repentance*, but *Requiem*'s epilogue, memorializing those who were left behind, seems a particular source of inspiration:

> There [in the queue] I learned how faces fall apart,
> How fear looks out from under the eyelids,
> How deep are the hieroglyphics
> Cut by suffering on people's cheeks.

A few lines later:

> And I pray not only for myself,
> But for all who stood there
> In bitter cold, or in the July heat,
> Under that red blind prison-wall.

And very near the poem's conclusion, Akhmatova specifies the site of any monument erected to her in the future: not in her birthplace by the sea, nor in Tsarskoe Selo where she triumphed as a poet:

> But here, where I stood for three hundred hours
> And where they never, never opened the doors for me.[6]

We see Nino and Keti, waiting 'three hundred hours', before the doors that would 'never, never' open.

Another important literary allusion is to the Georgian national poem, *The Knight in the Panther s Skin*, which Sandro mentions as a pointed rebuke to Varlam when they are discussing whether or not 'the people' need re-education. This poem is absolutely central to Georgian cultural identity. It was written by Shota Rustaveli (ca. 1166–?) in the Golden Age of Georgian history, sometime during the marriage of Queen Tamara to Davit Soslan (1189–1207).[7] *The Knight in the Panther s Skin* is first and foremost a romance, but it is also political, celebrating the virtues of enlightened rule. Rustaveli ends the epic this way:

> They [the three sovereigns] poured upon all alike their mercy, like snowflakes from heaven.
> The orphans and the widows, the helpless and the poor were enriched, made happy.
> Evil-doers dared not appear but recoiled and vanished.
> Harmony reigned, like sheep, goat, and wolf fed together.[8]

Sandro is obviously implying that Georgia's national bard would have disapproved of Varlam Aravidze's methods of rule and ideas about art.

As important as these references are, most of the literary allusions in *Repentance* illuminate Varlam's character (rather than Sandro's or Nino's). For example, Varlam quotes Confucius (or so he claims) when he announces that 'It's difficult to catch a black cat in a dark room.' Varlam goes on to embellish Confucius by adding:

> We are faced by a most difficult task, but nothing can deter us. If we want to, we'll catch the black cat in the dark room, *even if there s no cat there*. [emphasis added]

This bit of dialogue most likely alludes as well to Bulat Okudzhava's well-known political song *The Black Cat*, in which Stalin was the black cat—not to mention the black cat in Mikhail Bulgakov's *The Master and Margarita*, an expert in assuming a variety of guises and at disappearing and reappearing at will.

Varlam frequently demonstrates his command of the rhetorical flourishes of Stalin-speak. 'Intimate boudoir art', he tells Sandro, is an 'escape from reality'. Varlam, like Stalin, is adept at verbal juggling acts, as when he informs Korisheli that he had (sadly) acceded to the will of the people by arresting 'his relative' Sandro: 'He's our foe, and we're his victims'. The few times in the film that Varlam speaks Russian (with a heavy Georgian accent, like Stalin's) are especially noteworthy examples of Stalin-speak. For example, Varlam tells Sandro, without a trace of irony, that 'modesty is a fine quality in a man'. Stalin thought so too.

This connection between Varlam and Stalin is further reinforced, as Anna Lawton has noted, by reference to Yevgeny Yevtushenko's famous poem from the Thaw, *The Heirs of Stalin* (1962).[9] In this case the quotations are visual, rather than verbal: we may compare the Varlam who will not stay buried to Stalin on his way to lie mummified beside Lenin in the mausoleum. Yevtushenko describes the 'awesome and mute' Stalin in his coffin this way:

Grimly clenching
his embalmed fists,
he watched through a crack inside,
just pretending to be dead.
He wanted to fix each pallbearer
in his memory: [...]
in order somehow later
to collect strength for a sortie,
and rise from the earth
and get
to them
the unthinking.
He has worked out a scheme.
He's merely curled up for a nap.

And several lines later:

It seems to me
a telephone was installed in the coffin.
To someone once again
Stalin is sending his instructions...
No, Stalin did not die.
He thinks death can be fixed.[10]

Despite the remarkable resemblance of these poetic images to the filmic Varlam, there can be no doubt that the most important literary reference in *Repentance* is Shakespeare's Sonnet 66. Varlam recites the sonnet from memory when he visits the Baratelis, and in its entirety— save for the last two lines. This sonnet, which is not particularly well-known, is absolutely critical to an informed understanding of the film. Varlam has already revealed the cultured side of his complicated persona to the Baratelis in his musical performance, but the recitation of Shakespeare is quite the most unexpected event of that fateful evening *chez* Barateli. (And for English-speakers, hearing Shakespeare in the rhythms of the mellifluous Georgian language is quite a treat.)

> Tired with all these for restful death I cry,
> As to behold desert a beggar born,
> And needy nothing trimm'd in jollity,
> And purest faith unhappily forsworn,
> And gilded honor shamefully misplaced,
> And maiden virtue rudely strumpeted,
> And right perfection wrongfully disgraced,
> And strength by limping sway disabled,
> And art made tongue-tied by authority,
> And folly, doctor-like, controlling skill,
> And simple truth miscall'd simplicity,
> And captive good attending captain ill,

(Varlam omits the final two lines):

> Tired with all these, from these I would be gone,
> Save that, to die, I leave my love alone.[11]

Within the cycle of Shakespeare's sonnets, number 66, with its 'schematic list of grievances' and its preoccupation with the world's basic injustice, has links to others with similar themes, as well as to Hamlet's 'To be or not to be' speech. On its own, however, and particularly without the last two lines that humanize and soften its tone of dull resentment, the sonnet stands as a catalogue of antitheses of virtues and their inversions.[12] Each abstract noun—faith, honor, virtue, perfection, strength, art, truth—is defeated by a subjectless past participle and adverb—unhappily forsworn, shamefully misplaced, rudely strumpeted, etc. That Varlam should recite this particular sonnet seems ironic indeed, given that he wields the authority that tongue-ties art, and his 'captain ill' demands the attendance of 'captive good'.

In sum, Shakespeare appears to have prophesied Stalinism and its attack on 'gilded honor', 'purest faith', and 'simple truth' more than three centuries before the fact. The expression on Sandro's face at the end of the recitation makes it clear that he at last understands that he is powerless before the evil that Varlam represents.

Filmic Techniques

Purely cinematic devices, as detailed in our frame analysis, also play an important role in reinforcing the surrealism that is central to Abuladze's style. The color in the film is dense and vibrant. (Since the movie was originally made for television, watching it on video actually provides an excellent sense of the intensity of the color saturation.) The color is in marked contrast to the pallid, washed-out palette of most Soviet films of the late Brezhnev era—and certainly in contrast to the grayness of Soviet life. For most Soviet audiences watching the film at time of first release, the jolts of color would have been particularly noticeable and 'foreign' in their stylishness. (Residents of Tbilisi, on the other hand, were by Soviet standards almost Italian in their sense of style.)

Moreover, the visually striking red-black-white color scheme (that of the Georgian national flag) that rears throughout the film suggests thematic connotations as well. In contrast to the black-robed judges and business-suited men, Keti and Guliko, the two moral opponents within the film's 'present', both appear in the courtroom in outfits dominated by white. The luxuriant red carnations that blanket Varlam's coffin reappear in the bouquet Riktafelov hands to Nino and in those that droop in a vase on Varlam's secretary's desk. Nino's richly red robe, a mantle worthy of a queen, or indeed a Madonna, acts as a visual symbol of her warmth and maternal love; it disappears after Sandro's arrest. The same colors, woven into a characteristic Caucasus pattern, are visible in the rug hanging behind Varlam in the Barateli apartment.

In terms of editing, the takes are several minutes long (making a long film feel even longer, especially for Western viewers accustomed to the rapid montage of television advertising or MTV). Quick cutting and noticeable camera movement are rare, except in the first three scenes. There the jump cuts reinforce the viewer's uncertain sense of what is going on. One good example from the beginning of the film is the cut from a close-up of the newspaper obituary notice to the flowers on Varlam's casket. Another is the cut from the mourners singing *Samshoblo* to a close-up of Guliko's face, to flowers on the path, etc. (During the opening shots of the funeral procession, camera placement is low, so that we are at eye level with the coffin being carried down the stairs, a rather unsettling perspective.)

The use of the close-up, especially the extreme close-up, *before* rather than *after* the perspective has been established, is an effective way to make the audience realize from the opening moments that this is not a Hollywood film. The first shot in the film is one such example of Abuladze's aesthetic of the extreme close-up: a woman's hands making something—which turns out to be a marzipan flower—*on* something— which turns out to be an elaborate cake.

Now that the major components of the film have been disassembled and subjected to first examination, we may move on to attempt interpretation. Clearly the film is strongly anti-authoritarian. It celebrates culture over technology, history over politics, humanity over ideology, spirituality over progress. But can this profoundly surrealistic film teach us anything that is worth knowing about *history*?

Notes

1   Tatiana Khloplyankina, 'On the Road That Leads to the Truth' in Michael Brashinsky and Andrew Horton, *Russian Critics on the Cinema of Glasnost*, (Cambridge: Cambridge University Press, 1994), p. 51.

2   Igor Aleinikov, 'Between the Circus and the Zoo', in Brashinsky and Horton, *Russian Critics*, p. 56. Aleinikov finds them so obvious as to be like 'highlighted sentences and blinking pointers'.

3   Joan Neuberger, e-mail to Denise J. Youngblood, January 1999.

4   'About the Past for the Sake of the Future' [*O proshlom dlia budushchego*], *Literaturnaia gazeta*, 25 February 1987, in Viktor Bozhonovich (ed.) *Pokaianie*, (Moscow: 1988), p. 16.

5   Julie Christensen, 'Tengiz Abuladze's *Repentance* and the Georgian Nationalist Cause', *Slavic Review* Vol. 50, no. 1 (Spring 1991), p. 166.

6   Anna Akhmatova, *'Requiem and 'Poem without a Hero* , trans. D. M. Thomas, (Athens: Ohio University Press, 1976), pp. 31–2.

7   Donald Rayfield, *The Literature of Georgia: A History*, (Oxford: Clarendon Press, 1994), pp. 73–4.

8   Shota Rustaveli, *The Knight in the Panthers Skin*, trans. Venera Urashadze, (Tbilisi: Sabchota Sakartvelo, 1971), p. 221. There is also a prose translation of this poem into English: Rustaveli, *The Lord of the Panther Skin*, trans. R. M. Stevenson, (Albany NY: State University of New York Press, 1977).

9   Anna Lawton, *Kinoglasnost: Soviet Cinema in Our Time*, (Cambridge: Cambridge University Press, 1992), p. 157.

10 Yevgeny Yevtushenko, 'The Heirs of Stalin', trans. George Reavey, in Yevtushenko, *The Collected Poems, 1952–1990*, ed. Albert C. Todd (ed.) with the author and James Ragan, (New York: Henry Holt, 1991), pp. 113–15.

11 William Shakespeare, 'Sonnet 66', in *The Complete Works of Shakespeare*, Cambridge edition text, William Aldis Wright (ed.), (New York: Doubleday, 1936), Vol. 1, p. 412.

12 David K. Weiser, *Mind in Character: Shakespeares Speaker in the Sonnets*, (Columbia MO: University of Missouri Press, 1987), p. 72. Weiser persuasively argues, on p. 73, that the last lines of the sonnet suggest that love 'sustains the speaker and suggest[s] that personal relations can compensate for all the world's dishonesty. Love survives the destruction of all other ideals, because it is a personal rather than a conventional value'.

4. The History That Is History

When a special screening of *Repentance* was arranged in 1987 for the Moscow intelligentsia, with director Tengiz Abuladze present, a critic introduced the film by quoting Lev Tolstoy, arguably the most historically-minded of the great Russian novelists: 'We say, why remember? Why remember the past? It's no longer with us, so why recall it? What do you mean, why remember?'[1] These are still potent and pertinent questions when considering the significance of this film. As we have already seen, *Repentance* is a film with so many meanings that it resists a single, privileged interpretation. Even if we admit that no single interpretation of the picture can ever hope to be privileged, the most interesting interpretations of this movie are in important respects *historical*. *Repentance* represents history within history within history.

Repentance in the Career of Tengiz Abuladze

We will work on unravelling the multiple strands of historicity in the film by moving from the individual—Tengiz Abuladze—to the general—the fate of humanity in the twentieth century. Born in 1924, Abuladze somehow avoided military service in World War II, spending the years 1943–6 at the Rustaveli Theater Institute in his native Georgia.[2] He next attended VGIK, the prestigious All-Union State Institute of Cinematography in Moscow, where he studied with Sergei Yutkevich.

After his graduation in 1953 (the year Stalin died), Abuladze filmed documentaries on Georgian life with his longtime friend from the Rustaveli Institute and VGIK, Georgian director Revaz Chkheidze (who later became head of Gruziafilm, the Georgian film studio, a position he held at the time of *Repentance*'s production).[3] Many of

Abuladze's movies from the Fifties and early Sixties paid homage to the impressive traditions of Georgian cinema, beginning with the film he co-directed with Chkheidze, *Magdana s Donkey* [*Lurdzha Magdany*, 1955].

His solo directorial debut, *Someone Else s Children* [*Chuzhie deti*, 1958], however, was a controversial psychological drama set in the present day. Indeed, it faithfully recounted an incident reported in *Komsomol skaia pravda*, about a woman who married a man she did not love for the sake of his children, and stayed with the children even after her husband abandoned her for another woman. The film took first prize for debut films at the 1960 London Film Festival and found a few defenders. Yutkevich, for instance, a highly-respected director of the older generation (and Abuladze's mentor at VGIK), praised Abuladze's efforts to avoid clichés, and attributed the film's flaws to the director's inexperience.[4] But orthodox critics, although they recognized Abuladze's adroit handling of landscape and *mise-en-scène*, disliked the 'absence of a clear ideological focus'.[5] Sergei Gerasimov, a powerful figure in the cinema world, condemned Abuladze's film as a 'sham imitation', inspired not by life but rather by film imitations of life. With its 'spiritual debility and incomprehension of the new socialist world', *Someone Else s Children* was 'alien' to Soviet values (a damning indictment); it was—worse yet—'effeminate cinema' (*zhenstvennoe kino*)![6]

In 1963 Abuladze directed *Grandmother, Iliko, Ilarion, and I* [*Ia, babushka, Iliko i Ilarion*], a rather banal comic presentation of the 'fathers and sons' relationship set before and during World War II, in which the elderly Ilarion and the young hero Zuriko are rough equals. Although several films and novels of the early Sixties managed to animate this familiar theme with the use of verbal or visual irony, Abuladze treats it straight. When Zuriko goes off to Tbilisi for schooling, for example, a voice-over characterizes the student years as 'the best years'; he returns to his village just in time to kiss his grandmother—whose work is now completed—before she dies, and he marries his true love Mary. The war itself is wholly extraneous, its intrusion into peacetime life shown via a familiar 'farewell' scene (although the usually perceptive film critic Maya Turovskaya praised Abuladze's laconic treatment of it, as well as the film's 'distinctively Georgian' quality).[7]

Grandmother, Iliko, Ilarion and I and Abuladze's 1965 *Svan Sketches* [*Svanskie zarisovki*, referring to the Georgian province of Svanetia], both exploit the Georgian countryside and a specifically Georgian tradition of comic types. But Abuladze first engaged seriously with the Georgian past in his beautiful and artistic black-and-white film *The Prayer* [*Molba*, 1968], a morality play set in medieval Georgia. *The Prayer* revealed Abuladze to be a student of history who was interested in bringing the texture and values of the past (rather than just the facts) to the screen. The second film in the self-proclaimed Georgian historical trilogy, *The Tree of Desire* [*Drevo zhelania*, 1977], appeared nine years later.[8] *The Tree of Desire* won numerous prizes at film festivals in the Soviet Union and in the West, at last establishing Abuladze as a major international director.[9] Between pictures, Abuladze was living in Tbilisi, teaching at his first alma mater, the Rustaveli Institute, and, we may safely assume, dreaming about whether it would ever be possible to make a film about the Stalin Terror in Georgia.

Finally the time seemed right for the venture. The period between inception and realization for *Repentance* was short. Abuladze began working on the script in 1981 and finished in it 1982; he shot the film over the course of five months (entirely on location and in real interiors) and finished it in December 1984. The production schedule was interrupted by the arrest and eventual execution of one of the original cast members for hijacking a plane, certainly an inauspicious sign.[10]

Abuladze credited Georgia's then Party Secretary, Eduard Shevardnadze, for suggesting that the film be made for Georgian television, thus bypassing the worst bureaucratic channels. Georgian television enjoyed a three-hour daily time slot reserved for local broadcasting, which was free of the oversight of Gosteleradio, the Soviet central television and radio agency.[11] Gruziafilm's distance from Moscow helped as well: official support for ethnic cultures permitted a certain measure of autonomy to regional studios. Even so, *Repentance* was not aired until 1986, a pivotal year for the arts in the Soviet Union, as discussed in the Introduction.

Brezhnev's death in 1982 ended the so-called 'era of stagnation'. Even though Brezhnev's successor, Yuri Andropov, had been Soviet ambassador to Hungary in 1956 when the tanks rolled in and later became head of the KGB, he proved to be something of a reformer in his short tenure as Party Secretary before he succumbed to kidney disease in 1984. 'The Periphery'—especially the Baltics, Ukraine and the nations of the Caucasus—began to stir at this time, hoping for increased cultural autonomy, if not full political independence. In

Georgia, Shevardnadze became an important patron of cultural–nationalist artists like Abuladze. Nonetheless, the production seemed ill-starred from the beginning, as when the hijacking scandal noted above scared Gruziafilm boss Chkheidze into stopping the production temporarily. (*Repentance*'s final version did little to soothe Chkheidze's concerns.)[12] It would not be long, however, before this Georgian film became famous far beyond the borders of the Transcaucasus. *Repentance* came to symbolize glasnost in cinema not only for the entire Soviet Union, but also for the world.

Repentance in the Context of the Times

In the perfervid atmosphere of glasnost, *Repentance* exploded like a Roman candle. In the final three months of 1986, Moscow's artistic and intellectual elite packed into exclusive venues like the Writers' Union club, the House of Cinema and the Artists' Union, the only sites where the film was screened at that point. Dissident Marxist historian Roy Medvedev anticipated the general release of *Repentance* as 'the most important event in Soviet cultural life in at least a decade'.[13] Excitement fizzed, spilling over in articles and reviews that forewarned ordinary viewers of the momentous experience in store for them. They had the opportunity to judge for themselves in 1987, when *Repentance* was commercially distributed. And judge they did, voting with their feet—some 30 million tickets were sold, an exceptionally large number for a 'difficult' picture, though theaters were often half-empty by the time the lights came up.[14] Spectators filled out survey questionnaires, and they also wrote letters to the press.

The following excerpts and paraphrases of professional criticism and popular responses typify the predominantly political *cum* moral response that *Repentance* elicited, whether appreciative or hostile. The first, translated almost in its entirety, was written by a man who himself symbolized and embodied the spirit of the men and women of the Sixties, the *shestidesiatniki*. As deputy to Alexander Tvardovsky, *Novyi mir*'s legendary editor in the Sixties, Vladimir Lakshin had strongly defended Alexander Solzhenitsyn's *One Day in the Life of Ivan Denisovich* when it came under attack in early 1964.[15] Lakshin continued to press passionately for greater candor and truthfulness, right up until he lost his job in the 1970 purge of *Novyi mir*'s entire liberal staff, which also removed Tvardovsky as editor.[16]

V. Lakshin, 'Unforgiving Memory' [Neproshchaiushchaia pamiat'], *Moskovskie novosti*, 30 November 1986

... I will say plainly: I am not a big fan of 'avant-garde' cinema, of surrealism, of ambiguous symbolism. But here the provocative jumble of an epoch is not distracting, it actually conveys ideas more forcefully. When does the action occur? Never and always. Where? Nowhere, everywhere. Everywhere laws are flouted and human individuality is trampled; everywhere terror, denunciations and fear become the normal condition of society.

... for a specific likeness in Varlam Aravidze's ... The film-makers ... they are telling us is ... gh older people recall ... , comes close to docu- ... remembers the cruel ... witnessed the criminal

... knows who, but that's ... ial power, based not on ... ways the same. If you ... , it's easy to understand ... Varlam a madman, a ... artist, he investigates the ... people from the involun-

... to a demonic changing of masks. To 'simple' people he appears as the benevolent city father. He is a generous Maecenas to the artist, a singer and declaimer of Shakespeare to the woman. Others carry out all the arrests, torture and executions without his knowledge, probably those same wicked people who are so ready to denounce one another, or unworthy members of his entourage ...

But the significance of *Repentance* is not confined to the figure of Varlam, and to scenes of terror. What lies at the center of the film reveals its contemporary ethical resonance: not crime, but punishment; not 'sin', but repentance. In essence, repentance is achieved twice in the film, but the first time it is incomplete, false, akin to self-justification. Abel confesses to a holy father whose face is hidden in

the gloom and whose hands, illuminated by candlelight, voluptu-
ously strip the flesh from a smoked fish. Abel is distressed, no longer
able to distinguish good from evil. A familiar, mocking laugh unexpectedly interrupts his confession: from the murk Varlam's satanic
face emerges, and the father informs the son that what's troubling
him is loneliness.

Genuine, profound repentance can occur only after profound
upheaval, after expiatory sacrifice. Just such an upheaval awaits
Abel, and it comes from an unanticipated and most painful source.
The adolescent who looks straight at us with clear, pure eyes had
questioned his father about the crimes attributed to his grandfather,
and his father readily rationalized: 'It was the times', 'enemies were
everywhere', 'mistakes happen'... What could the boy do when his
father's lies were exposed? Abel comprehends fully only after the
death of his son, his heir—and his second repentance is complete
and unconditional...

This picture has a special significance for our art. Tengiz Abuladze
develops this painful and unresolved theme with total artistry, an
artist who is both ruthless and unwilling to despair. Do we need
such a bitter, cruel memory of mistakes and crimes? That's what
Repentance is really asking. It replies: yes, we do. Without memory,
we will never move on, and we risk once more becoming the victims
of tragic errors and experiences we have not overcome ...

I am certain that the release of *Repentance* will be a significant
milestone for Soviet cinema and for cinema everywhere. Let the
reader not count my words an overstatement. So much has been
praised indiscriminately that one does not know what words to use
when a phenomenon appears in our cinema that will compel so
many people to ponder and reconsider, that will rock them with the
force of a spiritual earthquake.

The following excerpt expresses a more explicitly instrumentalist
approach to *Repentance*, as might be expected from a piece appearing in
Pravda.

G. Kapralov, 'Rejection of Evil' [Ottorzhenie zla], *Pravda*, 7
February 1987

... Many of those who watch the film today recall those years. The
country was in the thick of construction projects, astonishing the

world with the enthusiasm of millions who were ready to endure and overcome any hardship in the name of the victory of the Communist ideal. And whatever failed to conform seemed somehow awkward, an error that would correct itself at any moment ... [Tornike's suicide] is a warning to all the Abels, to all those who even now fear publicity, who fear the truth, the light of justice and the authentic socialist democracy that can control any and every Varlam ... Revolutionary processes are now taking place in our country. Lofty national ideals of humanism and democracy, of a genuine socialist revitalization, are inspiring the party and the whole nation. The film *Repentance* ... is both a sign of the times, and itself a fact of the moral purification of society, of courageous openness.

The following appeared in a biweekly film magazine that combined 'fan-mag' photomontages with thoughtful analyses and informative essays.

B. Vasil'ev, '(In)sight' [Prozrenie], *Sovetskii ekran*, June 1987

This film is about the murder of everything. People, conscience, friendship, honor, dignity, talent, goodness. And although there are no whips in it, I have the physical sensation of being scourged, I hear the hiss, I see not one individual but an entire people under the lash, herded into stalls, driven into madness, into a phantasmagorical medieval everyday reality.

This film is about philistine hatred. Toward culture and its creators, toward spiritual values, toward a nation's past. Hatred like this not only destroys: it plays the fool, it mocks, it acts out a vaudeville with many costume changes.

This film is about the continuity of evil. About a cancer-ridden society and spiritual metastases that taint subsequent generations. About evil's seduction, evil's governance, evil's retribution, evil's solace ...

After their deaths [dictators] decompose among the living, whether they were buried with thunderous cannon-blasts or doused with gas and set alight. Their corpses stink to this day, a stench that animates the bombings and assassinations in Italy and perfumes swastika-waving mobs in West Germany. In our own society the fetid regurgitations of Great Russian chauvinism and of regional nationalism stink of that same corpse. So does the nostalgia of retired lackeys for a 'strong personality'; so do the portraits of the Leader treasured by young people who know very little about the past . . .

A deafening explosion—Varlam Aravidze has destroyed the temple [church]. For me, symbol and reality blur: I remember another temple, destroyed in another city by someone else's order. Once upon a time it towered above the Moscow River, crowning the Boulevard Ring. The Cathedral of Christ the Savior, funded by voluntary contributions, commemorated the War of 1812; its most important battles and the names of its fallen heroes adorned the marble corridor that encircled that magnificent building. NAMES. It was an eternal flame in grateful memory of those who saved our fatherland. But an actual Varlam Aravidze scattered the ash of memory, and gratitude, and those heroic names. .. Thus film implodes into fact. But it goes further, revealing the reasons and the consequences of the calculated destruction of temples on our soil, temples in our culture and in each one of us . . .

In lieu of temples, simulacra appear: icing temples open and close the film. Sugared steeples, frosting churches, marzipan crosses—and no one protests. On the contrary: Varlam Aravidze got what he wanted, he relocated the temples from the spiritual domain to the digestive organs.

Again, this is not merely a brilliant metaphor. It is also a historical reality. We transformed churches into storehouses for fuel, into shops, or simply abandoned them; we placed prisons and labor camps in monasteries. And then, suddenly, we caught ourselves, and tried to save what remained. But we could save only the buildings, turning them into decorative tourist attractions where boys and girls dressed à la Russe to demonstrate Russian hospitality in exchange for foreign currency. . .

'What good is a road if it doesn't lead to a temple?' [actually 'church']—the old lady wonders . . . For me, that is the film's saddest and most important question: when, members of the intelligentsia, will you rebuild for the people that lost road to the temple? That's your mission, after all—to light a torch for the people, even if it scorches your hands and soul, to shed light till the last moment of your life and you pass on the torch . . . Has the stench of the past so befouled you that all you can do is dream of justice and fashion gingerbread temples for today's Abels?

Abuladze's film is a tocsin, summoning us to repent, a clarion call to our collective conscience. Enough! Enough lies, enough toadying, enough cowardice. Let us remember, finally, that we are all citizens. Proud citizens of a proud land.

Many non-professional viewers echoed the critics. According to a survey conducted in Tbilisi theaters by the Center of Public Opinion, under the auspices of the Central Committee of the Georgian Communist Party, most respondents characterized *Repentance* as an 'honest' film that 'candidly reflected what is negative in and alien to' their lives. Intellectuals regarded the film as creating 'a collective image of evil'; workers said that it presented essential contemporary problems.[17]

Soon after the film's commercial release, the Soviet Union's central institute for film research, VNIIK, commissioned a study of films as indicators of perestroika. *Repentance* was the first film selected for study, and researchers surveyed audiences in Moscow and Liubertsy, the latter a provincial town more representative of national reaction. At a time when two-thirds of moviegoers were under the age of 30, and one-quarter was between 30 and 50, *Repentance* found—or created—a statistically unusual audience: only one-third were under 30, and one-quarter over 50. In Moscow, three-quarters of those surveyed had some level of higher education.[18] About half those surveyed agreed with critics and considered *Repentance* successful: 49 per cent of younger viewers, who were the most excited by the film; 43 per cent of the 'middle-aged' group; 41 per cent of the older generation. Social position differentiated reactions even more than age: 59 per cent of respondents from the scientific intelligentsia and from the humanities agreed with the critics, in contrast to only 37 per cent of civil servants and bureaucrats and 37 per cent of workers.[19]

While audiences responded far less uniformly positively than did critics, the nature of those positive reactions was quite similar. One viewer wrote on the VNIIK questionnaire:

A marvelous film. Finally a spade is called a spade. We need more movies like this, so people will stop behaving like robots and our children and grandchildren will find the road to the Temple.

Another echoed *Pravda*:

The film matters today. Our society has embarked on a new stage of development. It's essential to understand that only free people can create a healthy society.[20]

A few months later *Sovetskii ekran* published a round-up of reader responses to the Vasil'ev piece cited above. Again, laudatory comments duplicated those of the critics. A young student in Minsk wrote:

> I watched *Repentance* and am still in shock. It's about our grand-fathers, our fathers, ourselves, about their time and ours as well, since theirs leads to ours, as ours will lead on to the next, and so forever ... Please, more movies like this! They're a breath of fresh air, they make us think. If we don't think, ask questions, we won't be able to teach our children, and there will be no guarantee that history, when it repeats itself as it always does, will not return to such bloody, medieval murk.[21]

Repentance elicited two types of negative response. In the VNIIK survey, non-Muscovites and members of the older generation were more likely to reject Abuladze's depiction of the Soviet past; in Liubertsy and elsewhere, members of the audience walked out of theaters before the film ended.[22] (One theater manager, hoping to forestall such departures by preparing her audiences for what they were about to see, replaced the short that would normally have preceded the feature with a ten-minute tape of discussions with people who had seen the film.) Older viewers understood the film as an allegory of what they themselves had lived through, but 'not all identified themselves with [the accused]' at the trial. Some reacted with irritation and even hostility: 'Truth, half-truth, lies. The film should not be shown'; 'The film is brilliantly made, but what for? Simply to say that nothing was ever any good here?'; 'Do we really need to stir up the past? There's sense to the proverb, "Corpses belong in the graveyard"'; 'It's hard to take. What do we need it for? Let those people whom it deals with watch it'; 'It's criminal to pay people for work like that.'[23]

A very different sort of negative response came from those who repudiated Abuladze's stylistic choices. 'I didn't like the picture', one of VNIIK's respondents wrote, continuing:

> The mixture of comedy and tragedy. A real hodge-podge. Several corpses, but no sympathy. Some kind of explanation should precede

the film. I did stay till the end, but mainly because of the acting, the music and the visual beauty [*krasochnost*].[24]

On a rather more sophisticated level, letter-writers to *Sovetskii ekran* concurred: 'Right now we need analytic films, without metaphor and symbol', wrote a woman from Yaroslavl. She went on:

> The plain, unadorned truth, where Stalin would be shown without the mask of a demigod who, twirling his moustache, hears out his generals and looks at us with a weary gaze. In my view, Abuladze overly generalizes the image of his dictator. First we need specifics, then we can generalize. The problem of the cult of personality is so massive that it cannot be resolved using Aesopian language.

A man from Penza echoed her objection: 'There's no need for Aesopian language, the perpetual language of a spiritually enslaved society, in an atmosphere of glasnost where the rule of law is guaranteed.' Igor Aleinikov, a Moscow film-maker who collaborated with his brother on several films of the 'alternative cinema' movement, agreed:

> The time for aesthetic realization of the 1930s material has not yet arrived. First call a spade a spade—otherwise historical issues will be clouded for general audiences.

Aleinikov angrily dismissed Abuladze's symbolic language as 'labels in a museum exhibit', playing pieces in a 'cheap and useless game'.[25]

The most thoughtful repudiation of *Repentance* came from a group of Moscow students:

> Who is Varlam Aravidze? A collective image of all tyrants from Nero until today? But then he is deprived of his specific social roots, and every tyrant is the product of historical circumstances. What produced Varlam? The film doesn't answer that question; it suggests that tyranny is an attribute of Destiny, inevitably spawned by humankind from time to time ... When Varlam appears before us he already commands power. Who gave him that power? The film emphasizes Varlam's personal qualities: his cruelty, his falseness, his demagogy. But those are only repugnant characteristics, they don't

represent a mandate for power. As a result the film treats an historical phenomenon, tyranny, as a blind stroke of fate. It's especially
painful when realistic episodes from our national history (the log
scene, the line of women at the prison window) appear to be ascri-
bed to inexplicable and inevitable historical phenomena. Does that
really answer our need for historical truth? In order to acknowledge
and rectify the mistakes of the past, is it really enough just to dig up
the corpse of one tyrant (or even all tyrants)? ... The film showed
what a tyrant can be like, but it failed to address the main issue:
how did such a tyranny come about?[26]

Overall, the release of *Repentance* won Gorbachev a great deal of credit
and trust among the liberal intelligentsia. It signalled Gorbachev's own
stance *vis-à-vis* the past, as well as toward relics of the Stalinist
mentality who were alive and well within the Party. For the disaffected
elite, the *shestidesiatniki* and their epigones, a genuine examination of
the past—especially of the Terror that carried off its parents and grand-
parents—was one, perhaps the only, way to revive some measure of
commitment, and despite their wariness and even skepticism, they
responded eagerly.

Repentance and Georgian History

Repentance has other histories as well, both national (Georgian) and
multi-national (Soviet/Stalinist). Abuladze's two previous important
works, *The Prayer* and *The Tree of Desire*, comprise a striking duet. They
are both remarkable visual tributes to the richness of folk culture and
spiritual life in Georgia long before Soviet power, and in the case of
The Prayer, before Russian imperial conquest, too. If *Repentance*, which
seems only tenuously related to *The Prayer* and *The Tree of Desire* in
visual and thematic terms, is indeed the third film in a trilogy, then
how does that fact affect the meaning of its predecessors? This is an
especially vexing question since Abuladze himself said that the idea of
Repentance first arose 20 years earlier, when he began work on *The
Prayer*.[27]

On the surface, *The Prayer* and *The Tree of Desire* celebrate the
fullness and drama of Georgia's storied culture and history, while
Repentance recounts its most shameful episode.[28] But the beauty and
mystery of *Repentance*'s predecessors do not mean that Abuladze

glossed over the darker sides of Georgian life. Indeed, *The Prayer* deals with danger, enmity, and mistrust. It is based on three epic poems by the beloved Georgian nationalist poet Vazha-Pshavela (the pen name of Luki Pavlis-dze Razikashvili, 1861–1915): *Aluda Ketelauri* (1888), *Host and Guest* (1893), and his masterpiece, *The Snake-Eater* (1901).[29] These poems explore themes of death, sacrifice and redemption in the Georgian heroic tradition,[30] which are, in Abuladze's words:

> the origins and murderous strength of evil, of prejudice and moral stagnation. The poet prays to God that the thirst for good will never desert him, that he will die unsatiated ... For Vazha there are no innocent and guilty in a relationship of hatred—the hatred itself is tragic. The film's action occurs 'never and always', simultaneously in legendary days of old and at the turn of the century.[31]

The Tree of Desire continues *The Prayer*'s theme, with its opening shots of an ominous shroud that obscures a spring-blossoming field, and the killing of a beautiful white horse, metaphor for the power of evil that carries across generations. Here Abuladze chose for his inspiration the work of another important Georgian writer, poet Giorgi Leonidze (1899–1966). (Leonidze, who cowered in fear of Beria during the Terror and who was known for the 'simulated verve' of his panegyrics to Stalin, wrote *The Tree of Desire* in 1956 as part of his own 'repentance'.)[32] Again Abuladze deals with the theme of destructive enmity and the violence perpetrated on the individual, expanding the motifs of *The Prayer* to include an exploration of the challenges that modernity, especially the turn-of-the-century Russian-inspired revolutionary movements, posed to traditional Georgian values. The heroine Marita falls in love with a poor boy, but she is married off to a man whom she does not love. No one wants to destroy Marita: on the contrary, as Abuladze has said, they all wish her well. Yet the village elder sacrifices her happiness for the welfare of the larger community. This action, which was justified in the name of the clan ('we're a small nation, we need healthy descendants, we'll give Marita up to a rich household, she'll be in good hands, we'll secure the future'), ends in the death of the heroine. *The Tree of Desire*, Abuladze commented, portrays anguish for a squandered harmony and calls for the restoration of that harmony, so integral to human nature.[33]

Blood, vengeance and sacrifice abound in both movies. As

Vazha-Pshavela vividly wrote in *Aluda Ketelauri*, one of the poems celebrating Georgian blood feuds that served as the basis of and narration for *The Prayer*.

> Whoever thirsts for enmity,
> Let his house door open wide,
> Let his heart be a dam of blood,
> Let his feet stand in the pool, ...[34]

Given this context of 'pools of blood', we must remember that the Stalin Terror, after all, was not something merely done *to* Georgians. It was done *by* them, as well.

The chief architects of the Terror were both low-born native sons of Georgia, steeped in the violent and vengeful traditions of the mountain warriors. The terrible deeds of Stalin (born Djugashvili) are well known to all and too numerous to repeat here. Those of his minion Lavrenti Beria, Party chief of the Transcaucasus during the Terror and later head of the secret police (then called the NKVD), are as infamous as Stalin's to Soviet citizens and especially to Georgians.[35] Abuladze never names either of them in the film, which would have been impossible even in the early Eighties, and also contrary to his desire to universalize his message. The dialogic and visual allusions to both men are, however, clearly represented in *Repentance*.

Abuladze most obviously reinforces the specifically Georgian aspects of this tragedy in the construction of the character of Varlam Aravidze. First, as we have already noted in the previous chapter, Varlam's manner of speaking is indistinguishable from Stalin's rhetorical style. Second, the well-known Georgian theater actor Avtandil Makharadze looks and acts so much like Beria (in his characteristic pince-nez glasses) when he is playing Varlam that some elderly Soviets told us Makharadze's brilliant impersonation resurrected long-dormant fears of the Thirties and Forties.[36] Like Beria, Varlam is an outsider in the social establishment. Additionally, Varlam frequently speaks in folksy Georgian cliches,[37] and when he visits the Barateli apartment, he wears 'native' costume, a dramatic Caucasian sheepskin cloak called the *burka*.

Abuladze expresses an intrinsically Georgian point of view in other ways as well. He cues the audience to this almost immediately (although Western and perhaps many Soviet spectators would have missed it), when the mourners at Varlam's funeral break into a rousing version of the Menshevik song *Samshoblo*. This scene can only be read as a symbol of Georgian resistance, not against Russians necessarily, and not against communism, but against *Bolshevism*, in the period 1918–21 and beyond. Perhaps we are to understand that as Bolsheviks, Stalin and Beria had abjured their nation. Certainly, Stalin had no patience with his countrymen's tendency toward particularism, and Georgia suffered greatly during the Terror. (Although Stalin's might remains a source of pride for some Georgians today, others regarded his excesses as peculiar to the Russian, not the Georgian, national character.)

Georgian historical and literary figures are occasionally mentioned over the course of the flashback. We have already discussed the meaning of the reference to Rustaveli's poem *The Knight in the Panther's Skin*, from which even ordinary Georgians memorized long passages.[38] But the film's main symbol of cultural and historic Georgianism is the Church, reminding us that Georgia was one of the first nations to become Christianized, through the efforts of St. Nino, in the fourth century. The film's opening scene shows Keti decorating her wedding cakes with spun-sugar cathedrals. The fact that the Church being abused as a scientific laboratory is an ancient one, dating from the sixth century, again serves to emphasize how venerable Georgian civilization is, much older than that of the Russians.

The implication is that Georgians have traded this true religion for the religion of science; remember that Marx called his own system 'scientific socialism', and the Bolsheviks carried the Marxist/positivist obsession with science to extraordinary extremes. Varlam says: 'So you're opposed to science and progress?' when Sandro makes his plea to save the Church, then quickly sets up 'history and pride' as the *antagonists* of 'science and progress'. (While Varlam agrees with Sandro that the Church is 'our history, our pride', unlike Sandro, he does not see these as particularly positive attributes.)

Even Varlam's ghost continues to mock Georgia's spiritual traditions. The apparition greedily and disgustingly devours the fish, symbol of Christianity, smearing it over his face, as he contemptuously dismisses his son Abel's struggles with his long-dormant conscience. Finally, Varlam's grandson Tornike seeks redemption for the family's honor through repentance and self-sacrifice (though Christianity does not, of course, condone suicide).

The story of the Church has yet another meaning in the context of the film. The misuse or outright destruction of churches in the Soviet period was common and well known, dating from the earliest days of the Revolution, but continuing with a vengeance in the anti-religious campaigns that were part of the Stalin Revolution (1928–32). The most infamous example was the 1931 destruction of the Cathedral Church of Christ the Savior in Moscow, in order to build the Palace of Soviets. (Because of construction problems, the cathedral was in fact replaced by what was claimed to be the world's largest outdoor swimming pool. Today, ironically, an exact replica of the cathedral has replaced the swimming pool!)

Numerous films were commissioned in the late Twenties and early Thirties on anti-religious topics. The most interesting of these was *Out of the Way!* [*Khabarda!*, 1931], made by the Georgian director, Mikhail Chiaureli, who became Stalin's favorite and directed some of the most notorious pictures in the cult of Stalin, including *The Fall of Berlin* [*Padenie Berlina*, 1949]. Abuladze's Church subplot is remarkably reminiscent of the plot of *Out of the Way!*, where the politically correct story of the destruction of a church to make way for a club is undercut by the ironic, tongue-in-cheek villainy of the historians and intellectuals who are fighting to save the church. *Out of the Way!* may be the only film from the anti-religious campaign that successfully incorporates moments of genuine, zany comedy into profoundly hateful subject matter. In an ambiguous tribute to *Out of the Way!*, *Repentance* also has its zany moments, especially at the beginning of the flashback, when Varlam insists on delivering his inaugural address despite the fact that a watermain in the square has broken, spraying water all over him, and making so much noise that no one can hear. A final, very curious Chiaurelian connection is that the elderly woman trying to find a church on Varlam Street at the movie's end is Veriko Andzhaparidze (1900–87), Chiaureli's wife and the star of many of his films.[39] *Repentance* may, therefore, serve in some respects as Abuladze's (and Andzhaparidze's) apology for Chiaureli's dubious contributions to the history of Georgian and Soviet cinema.

Repentance and Soviet History

Though Abuladze was unquestionably a Georgian cultural nationalist, he intended us to think beyond the narrowly parochial in the case of

Repentance. The first two films in his trilogy, *The Prayer* and *The Tree of Desire*, are indubitably more Georgian than Soviet. In *Repentance*, however, Abuladze was casting his net much more widely. As noted in the first chapter, 'Aravidze' means 'everyman' or 'any man' in Georgian, so Varlam could just as easily be construed as *Homo Sovieticus*, rather than as a specifically Georgian villain. In fact *Repentance* presents a remarkable history of the mentalities of the Stalin Terror, effectively demonstrating the 'realism of surrealism' at this historical moment.[40]

The Stalinist Terror was extraordinarily surrealistic. To read any of the great survivors' accounts—Evgenia Ginzburg's *Journey into the Whirlwind*, Lev Kopelev's *To Be Preserved Forever*, Gustav Herling's *A World Apart*, Varlam Shalamov's thinly fictionalized *Kolyma Tales*, not to mention Solzhenitsyn's *The Gulag Archipelago*—is to enter into the heart of darkness. There is literally nothing that happens in *Repentance*, however bizarre, that did not happen hundreds of thousands, even millions, of times from 1928 to 1953 (and earlier if one listens to the testimony in Marina Goldovskaya's powerful glasnost-era documentary *Solovki Power* [*Vlast solovetskaia*, 1988]).

The air of surrealistic disassociation from reality that was an essential part of the Great Terror is established at the very beginning of the flashback. Varlam stands on the balcony, drenched in water, giving a speech that no one can hear, while on the street below revellers carrying mannequins of 'enemies' in effigy bob energetically, as the child Keti innocently blows bubbles until Sandro pulls her away. (Varlam later tells Sandro, 'I notice everything, so beware of me. Some blow bubbles, while others track enemies of the people.')

The pure arbitrariness of the arrest of class enemies (like the elderly 'blue-bloods' Moise and Miriam) and accidental enemies (like the 'truckload of Darbaiselis' that Doksopoulo worked for a month to round up and arrest) was yet another hallmark of the terror. Korisheli managed to get Moise and Miriam released the first time, so the next time, if they are arrested and *not* released, well then, they must be guilty. And given that loyal, dimwitted Doksopoulo proudly labored to find all those Darbaiselis, would it not actually do more harm to the Cause to admit the mistake and let them go? (Varlam relented and allowed a joyous Doksopoulo to keep his prize.)

Varlam's attraction to artists and intellectuals like Sandro, coupled with his marked fear and suspicion of them, was also a hallmark of the times. (In this regard Varlam closely resembles Stalin, who decisively intervened in the fates of writers like Zamiatin, Pasternak, Bulgakov and Mandelstam.) Varlam wants to insinuate himself with Sandro, initially pretending to agree with him that the Church must be preserved. He even goes so far as to claim that they share a common ancestor (an assertion Varlam makes again, to Korisheli, after Sandro's arrest, implying that he never would have arrested a relative without just cause). But seconds later Varlam works himself into a rage, as he thinks of those 'sluts' and 'criminals' who oppose his vision of utopia. He screeches in Russian at the startled Sandro: 'How can this be normal?!'

We see similar contradictions in Varlam at the Barateli apartment. He appears to admire Sandro's paintings: 'This is the kind of art we need, serious, thoughtful, and deep'—but follows this immediately with an attack on 'intimate, boudoir art' that is an 'escape from reality'. Sandro, an unrepentant representive of the intelligentsia, refuses to yield to threats, whether direct or implied. He firmly rejects Varlam's suggestion that 'artists like you must be with us now'. Sandro does not want to be an 'artist in uniform'; he spurns the dictator's mentality that labels artists 'engineers of human souls'.

Varlam embodies the authoritarian subordination of individuality and freedom to society and order in other ways as well. After Sandro's arrest, Varlam tells Korisheli that he has been forced to 'fulfill the will of the people' to remove his 'relative' Sandro from society. Sandro has been denounced as a 'pompous artist', a 'hooligan', an 'individualist', an 'anarchist'. Korisheli, shocked, informs Varlam that it is the authors of such denunciations, not Sandro, who are the 'enemies of the people'. In one of the most important scenes in the flashback, Varlam replies that 'In this matter, I must support the majority', whereupon Korisheli seals his own fate by angrily retorting, 'One intelligent person is worth one thousand idiots'. When Varlam smugly informs Korisheli that '[Sandro]'s our foe, and we're his victims', Korisheli strikes him hard in the face, breaking Varlam's pince-nez glasses. But it hardly matters, since Varlam can't 'see' with them anyway. As Soviet sociologist L. G. Ionin put it in his 1987 critique of *Repentance*, 'Varlam is the incarnation of absolute non-individuality, of total death'.[41]

Lastly, the growing hysteria that led people to believe just about any plot, rumor or accusation, no matter how improbably 'irrational', is brilliantly illustrated. Korisheli's admission that he was the leader of a

vast conspiracy to poison corn and dig transcontinental (and transo-
ceanic) tunnels is no more absurd than any of the numerous bogus
train wrecks, car accidents, assassination attempts and Trotskyite
conspiracies that the Old Bolsheviks confessed to at their travesties of
trials in the Thirties.[42] Nor is Varlam's speech from his balcony after
Sandro's interrogation 'fantasy' more than slightly overwrought: 'We
must be vigilant and prepared to unmask enemies', Varlam exhorts his
followers. 'Four out of every three persons are enemies. Numerically,
one enemy is greater than one friend'.

This type of mass hysteria, whipped up by the charismatic leader,
was certainly not unique to the Soviet Union in the mid-twentieth
century. With differing degrees of intensity and with national varia-
tions, we see it in Germany and Italy, in Japan and China, in the USA,
in the age of the dictators, racists, warmongers and red-baiters.
Abuladze hints at this by dressing Varlam most of the time in Beria-
chic, different from Stalin's more modest khaki. And at times,
especially in the speech noted above, Varlam adopts the shrill tones
and feverish gesticulations of Hitler or Mussolini. (Unlike them, Stalin
rarely appeared or spoke in public. His carefully crafted public persona
was that of a reasonable, reserved, soft-spoken man, as impersonated
by actors in the movies.) It is not unreasonable to assume that, despite
his stress on the particularities of the Georgian and Soviet contexts for
Repentance, Abuladze also wants us to understand that fascism is
fascism, whether in its red-draped or black- or brown-shirted varieties.

Repentance as 'History'

Whatever their broad implications, Abuladze's 'universalizing' details
are no more than a footnote to *Repentance*'s commentaries on the
relationship between Georgian culture and Soviet history in the
Thirties. As we hope we have also demonstrated, *Repentance*'s highly
stylized depiction of the Stalin Terror is brilliantly suited to the subject
matter. ('Absurd and fantastic reality,' Abuladze observed, 'requires
corresponding means of expression.')[43] But *Repentance* contributes in an
important and creative way to the genre of historical films in its
discourse on the relationship between society and history as developed
in the two framing stories.

The flashback alone profitably serves as a cinematic text for
Soviet history. That segment is *Repentance* at its most basic and

comprehensible. The framing stories, however, provide a more sophisticated rumination on the philosophy of history. Although in recent years historians have engaged in a more complex interrogation of film texts, interesting examples of which are collected in the anthologies edited by Robert Rosenstone (*Revisioning History*) and Vivian Sobchack (*The Persistence of History*), most historians are still firmly logocentric.[44] It is historio*graphy*, after all.

Repentance opens up new possibilities for the historical film, moving beyond facticity into an exploration of mentalities. *Repentance* is clearly an evocation of the various mentalities of the authoritarian Thirties, but it is also a thoughtful examination of the meaning of a troubled past to those who have survived it (like Keti and Abel) and those who have inherited it (like Tornike). For Keti in particular, history lives; as Yevtushenko concludes in *The Heirs of Stalin*:

> While the heirs of Stalin
> are still alive on this earth,
> it will seem to me
> that Stalin still lives in the mausoleum.[45]

Keti functions as historian, or the voice of collective, popular memory, from the very beginning of the movie. She will not let the past (personified by Varlam) be buried. Furthermore, she insists on giving voice to the past at her trial, transforming an inquiry into her 'crimes' into an inquiry into *society s* crimes. 'You must all want to know why I'm pursuing the deceased,' she says. '*I have no choice*' [emphasis added].

Abel, on the other hand, feels otherwise. He thinks he *has* a choice—and chooses to be silent, to pretend that he does not remember Keti, that he does not know what his father did. When Tornike demands: 'Did you know all that?', Abel is evasive: 'It's difficult to explain now ...'. Abel is puzzled and hurt by Tornike's anger; he plaintively asks his son: 'What am I guilty of?' To which Tornike responds: 'You justify Grandpa and follow in his footsteps.' From this point to the end of the film, Tornike continues to insist that Abel's silence is not merely misleading. It is, rather, an outright lie, a denial of the past, a refusal to accept responsibility for it, a failure to repent. Tornike's final words to his father before his suicide are: 'How can you go on lying forever?'

Tornike's atonement for his grandfather's crimes and his father's silence during his own life may seem misplaced, a spurious justification of the concept of collective guilt. We think, however, that Abuladze intended for us to accept Tornike's assumption of 'guilt' symbolically, rather than literally. Yevtushenko says that Stalin's heirs 'secretly consider their retirement temporary'.[46] Varlam's heirs, Abel and especially Guliko, scheme actively for a return to power. Until they repent, they are, in Yevtushenko's words, 'still alive on this earth'. This is what Keti means when she says at the end of her trial: 'Aravidze is not dead. He's alive and continues to corrupt society.' So who is sane and who is insane?, to paraphrase Tornike's final despairing cry.

This is not just a Georgian issue, nor is it just a Soviet issue. Debates over the sins of the past were at the heart of numerous culture wars at the end of the twentieth century. There seems no end to new evidence of complicity for the crimes of the Holocaust, as the Swiss bank account scandal of the late Nineties demonstrated. Many conservative Americans feel that the nation's once proud past has been transformed into a series of crimes: from the history that emphasized the discovery of America to the one that focuses on the extermination of the indigenous population; from the history that explored establishment of a free republic to the one that uncovers the misdeeds of the Founders; from the history that explained how America won the 'good war' to the one that focuses on Hiroshima and the internment of Japanese-American citizens.

Yevgeny Yevtushenko, who came to fame as the paradigmatic poet of the Khrushchev era's Thaw (the first epoch of glasnost), wrote often about de-Stalinization and the importance of bearing historical witness. In another work from 1962, *The Dead Hand of the Past*, he says:

Someone still untamed and restless
fiercely grips the hour hand
and, in striving to drag it down,
hangs on to history's clock.[47]

One of the most important and positive 'events' of the glasnost and perestroika era was that it provided the arena for a vigorous interrogation of the past, as R. W. Davies has described so well in his book *Soviet History in the Gorbachev Era*. Davies, who is not a film scholar and therefore has no particular reason to privilege a film over any of the other key documents of the era, notes at the very beginning of his work that it was *Repentance* that provided the spark for what he called the 'mental revolution'.[48] The hand clenching 'history's clock' was at last unloosed.

Notes

1 Quoted by Andrei Bitov in 'The Courage of an Artist', *Moscow News*, 15 February 1987. This same quotation appears in Teimuraz Mamaladze, 'Parable and Truth', in Robert Ehlers *et al.*, (eds.) *The USSR Today: Perspectives from the Soviet Press*, 7th edn (Columbus, Ohio: Current Digest of the Soviet Press, 1988), p. 170.

2 Biographical information comes from S. I. Yutkevich, (ed.), *Cinema: An Encyclopedic Dictionary* [*Kino: Entsiklopedicheskii slovar*], (Moscow: Sovetskaia entsiklopediia, 1986), p. 8.

3 Julie Christensen, 'Tengiz Abuladze's *Repentance* and the Georgian Nationalist Cause', *Slavic Review* Vol. 50, no. 1, (Spring 1991), p. 163.

4 'The Danger of Stereotypes' [Opasnost shtampy], *Iskusstvo kino* no. 2, (1960), p. 24.

5 Aleksandr Shtein, 'A Conversation with Friends' [Razgovor s druz'iami], *Iskusstvo kino* no. 3, (1959), p. 14.

6 Sergei Gerasimov, 'Reflections on the Young' [Razmyshlenniia o molodykh], *Iskusstvo kino* no. 2, (1960), p. 22. Gerasimov assailed the film for the first time when he chaired a Ministry of Culture discussion. His remarks on *Someone Else s Children* appear in a summary of his talk; see 'The Counterfeit and the Real' [Poddel'noe i podlinnoe], *Iskusstvo kino* no. 5, (1960), pp. 18–19.

7 Maya Turovskaya, '*Grandmother, Iliko, Ilarion* and the Movie Camera' [*Babushka, Iliko, Ilarion* i kinokamera], *Iskusstvo kino* no. 3, (1963), p. 16.

8 Two films appeared in 1972, a feature film, *A Necklace for My Beloved*, and a documentary, *Open Air Museum* (also titled *Dagestan*).

9 *The Tree of Desire* also established Abuladze as the spiritual and artistic cousin of the much beleaguered Georgian-Armenian director Sergo Paradzhanov, who spent much of the time after the 1965 sensation of his mystical film *Shadows of Our Forgotten Ancestors* incarcerated in mental institutions, supposedly for his sexual preferences.

10 The alleged hijacker, Georgii Kobakidze, had played the role of Tornike Aravidze. See Christensen, 'Tengiz Abuladze's *Repentance*', p. 163.

11 Anna Lawton, *Kinoglasnost: Soviet Cinema in Our Time*, (Cambridge: Cambridge University Press, 1992), pp. 154–5.

12 Christensen, 'Tengiz Abuladze's *Repentance*', p. 163.

13 *The Washington Post*, 31 October 1986.

14 A. Bogdanov and V. Vil'chek, '*Repentance* and 1000 Confessions' [*Pokaianie i 1000 ispovedei*], *Sovetskaia kul tura*, 9 April 1987, in Viktor Bozhovich, (ed.), *Pokaianie* (Moscow: 1988), p. 155. A viewer who wrote to Abuladze said much the same thing; in Bozhovich, p. 168.

15 Abraham Rothberg, *The Heirs of Stalin: Dissidence and the Soviet Regime*,

1953–1970, (Ithaca, New York and London: Cornell University Press, 1972), pp. 121–2.

16   Michael Scammell, *Solzhenitsyn: A Biography*, (New York and London, 1985), p. 685.

17   Cited by T. Mamaladze, 'Parable and Truth' [Pritcha i pravda], *Izvestia*, 30 January 1987; in Bozhovich, *Pokaianie*, p. 133.

18   Bogdanov and Vil'chek, '*Pokaianie* i 1000 ispovedei', p. 151.

19   Bogdanov and Vil'chek, pp. 152–3.

20   Bogdanov and Vil'chek, pp. 153, 154.

21   Tatiana Khloplyankina, 'The Alarm Tolls' [Pod zvuki nabatnogo kolokola], *Sovetskii ekran* no. 14 (6/1987), in Bozhovich *Pokaianie*, pp. 158–9.

22   One man wrote to Abuladze from Gorno-Altaisk: 'Without due reflection, one can dismiss the film as nonsense. And many did just that, while they watched and afterwards. One by one or a few at a time, viewers got up and walked out: when the lights came up, what had been a packed house was less than half full.' See 'Letters from Viewers' [Pis'ma zritelei], in Bozhovich, *Pokaianie*, p. 168.

23   Bogdanov and Vil'chek, '*Pokaianie* i 1000 ispovedei', p. 152.

24   Bogdanov and Vil'chek, p. 153.

25   Igor Aleinikov, 'Between the Circus and the Zoo' [Mezhdu tsirkom i zooparkom], *Cine-fantom*, nos 7/8 (1987); trans. in Brashinsky and Horton, *Russian Critics*, pp. 53, 56. (We have modified the translation slightly.)

26   Khloplyankina, 'Pod zvuki nabatnogo kolokola', pp. 160–1.

27   'Nowhere and Everywhere. Never and Always' [Nigde i vezde. Nikogda i vsegda], (Interview with Neya Zorkaya), *Novoe vremia*, 6 February 1987, in Bozhonovich, *Pokaianie*, p. 7.

28   The most comprehensive history of Georgia is that given in Ronald Grigor Suny, *The Making of the Georgian Nation*, 2nd edn, (Bloomington: Indiana University Press, 1994).

29   Rayfield, *Literature of Georgia*, p. 217.

30   For a brief biography of Vazha-Pshavela and analysis of his *oeuvre*, see Rayfield, *Literature of Georgia*, pp. 207–17; for information on his role in the Georgian cultural renascence of the nineteenth century, see Suny, *Making of the Georgian Nation*, p. 133.

31   'Nigde i vezde', p. 7.

32   Rayfield, *Literature of Georgia*, p. 290–1.

33   'Nigde i vezde' p. 11.

34   Rayfield, *Literature of Georgia*, p. 209; also quoted by Christensen in 'Tengiz Abuladze's *Repentance*', p. 170. Rayfield's chapter on Vazha-Pshavela includes many wonderful translations of the work of this extraordinary poet.

35   Suny's discussion of Stalinism in Georgia, and Beria's role in it, is particularly good; see *Making of the Georgian Nation*, pp. 260–91.

36   Janet Maslin, the doyenne of New York film critics, mistakenly claimed in her review of the film that Makharadze bore a stunning physical

resemblance to *Stalin*. See Maslin, '*Repentance*: A Satire from Soviet' [sic], *New York Times*, 4 December 1987.

37 Christensen, 'Tengiz Abuladze's *Repentance*', p. 169.

38 For a brief discussion of Rustaveli and *The Knight in the Panthers Skin*, see Suny, *Making of the Georgian Nation*, p. 39.

39 Julie Christensen notes that Andzhaparidze had previously played a key role in Abuladze's *The Tree of Desire*; see 'Tengiz Abuladze's *Repentance*', p. 174.

40 Denise J. Youngblood, '*Repentance*: Stalinist Terror and the Realism of Surrealism', in Robert A. Rosenstone (ed.), *Revisioning History: Film and the Construction of a New Past*, Princeton Studies in Culture, Power, and History, (Princeton, NJ: Princeton University Press, 1995), pp. 139–54. This section of this chapter reflects an expansion and rethinking of the ideas reflected in the earlier piece.

41 Quoted by R. W. Davies, *Soviet History in the Gorbachev Revolution*, (Bloomington: Indiana University Press, 1989), p. 91. Ionin's article appeared in *Sotsiologicheskie issledovaniia*, no. 3 (1987), pp. 62–72.

42 Robert Conquest details the madness of the era very well in *The Great Terror: A Reassessment*, (Oxford: Oxford University Press, 1990), especially in chapters 5–7.

43 'Nigde i vezde', p. 12.

44 Rosenstone (ed.), *Revisioning History*; Vivian Sobchack, *The Persistence of History: Cinema, Television, and the Modern Event*, (New York and London: Routledge, 1996).

45 Yevgeny Yevtushenko, *The Heirs of Stalin*, trans. George Reavey, in Yevtushenko, *The Collected Poems, 1952–1990*, (New York: Henry Holt, 1991), pp. 114–15.

46 Yevtushenko, *The Heirs of Stalin*, p. 114.

47 Yevtushenko, *The Dead Hand of the Past*, trans. George Reavey, in Yevtushenko, *Collected Poems*, p. 112.

48 Davies, *Soviet History*, p. 8.

Conclusion. 'The Dead Hand of the Past'[1]

Preoccupation with the legacy of history has been an obsession of the post-modern, post-World War II era. This is especially true at the start of not only a new century but a new millennium. The nineteenth-century faith in eternal progress now seems extraordinarily naive as we survey 100 years of war, genocide and authoritarianism.

Nowhere has this preoccupation with the past been more pronounced than in the former Soviet Union, the land where history was either denied or, as wags joked, endlessly changing. The bleak view of the Soviet past was best symbolized by the mourners at the seventieth anniversary 'celebration' of the Great October Revolution (in 1987) who carried a banner that carried the heartbreaking inscription '70 Years on the Road to Nowhere'. Or, as Keti says at the end of *Repentance*, 'This is Varlam Street. It will not take you to a church'. And the old lady asks, as she sadly walks away, 'Then what's the good of it?'

The cautionary answer that *Repentance* provides is a rather common-place one. There is no point in taking the path that leads away from history, culture, humanity and spirituality and towards the empty promises of utopia. If history can 'prove' anything by example, then surely the history of the twentieth century has proven that.

It seems to us, however, that Abuladze intended *Repentance* not so much as a warning, but as a challenge. The challenge for the survivors of the twentieth century is not to reconcile with the past, but as the film's title suggests, to *atone* for it. Whether we are 'guilty' or not (and Tornike surely was not guilty of anything), we have an obligation to the past. We are obligated to remember and to keep memory alive. As

Abel piteously weeps over his son's coffin, he cries in anguish: 'Why were you born, you fiend, Abel Aravidze?' Then, in his epiphany, Abel understands the answer: he was born to bear witness to his father's crimes, not to cover them up.

Abel's crime, therefore, was his silence. Through his silence, Abel has been history's greatest foe. By burying Varlam, he buried the past.

The era of glasnost and perestroika has not, unhappily, led to a better life for most of the citizens of the former Soviet Union, but it has led to the resurrection of history, both for good and for ill. The first glasnost, the period of Khrushchev's Thaw of the Fifties, proved abortive, even before Khrushchev's 1964 ousting. Yevgeny Yevtushenko's frustrations are most clearly expressed in the poem cited in the previous chapter, *The Dead Hand of the Past*. The censored fifth stanza of the poem reads:

> Dead hand of the past,
> You will not destroy the living.
> Dead hand of the past,
> We'll break your fingers' hold.[2]

Yevtushenko was not, even at the height of his glory, able to 'break [the] fingers' hold'. Twenty-five years later, Stalin's grip was finally broken through the efforts of artists like Abuladze, politicians like Gorbachev and thousands of extraordinary 'ordinary' citizens, but the battle is not yet won. *Repentance* is, and will forever remain, the cinematic symbol of that heroic struggle.

Notes

1 Referring to the eponymous poem in Yevgeny Yevtushenko, *The Collected Poems, 1952–1990*, (New York: Henry Holt, 1991), p. 112.

2 *Collected Poems*, p. 112. Translator George Reavey added this stanza from the original manuscript of the poem.

Further Reading

On the Stalinist Terror:

Robert Conquest *The Great Terror: A Reassessment*, Oxford: Oxford University Press, 1990.

On Georgian history and literature:

Donald Rayfield *The Literature of Georgia: A History*, Oxford: Clarendon Press, 1994.
Ronald Grigor Suny *The Making of the Georgian Nation*, 2nd edn Bloomington: Indiana University Press, 1994.

On Soviet popular culture:

Richard Stites *Russian Popular Culture: Entertainment and Society since 1900*, Cambridge: Cambridge University Press, 1992.

On Soviet cinema in the glasnost era:

Andrew Horton and Michael Brashinsky *The Zero Hour: Glasnost and Soviet Cinema in Transition*, Princeton, NJ: Princeton University Press, 1992.
Anna Lawton *Kinoglasnost: Soviet Cinema in Our Time*, Cambridge: Cambridge University Press, 1992.

For Soviet responses to Repentance:

Alexander Batchan 'Mad Russian', *Film Comment* Vol. 23, no. 3 (May/June 1987): p. 51.
Michael Brashinsky and Andrew Horton, (eds.), *Russian Critics on the Cinema of Glasnost*, Cambridge Studies in Film, Cambridge: Cambridge University Press, 1994.

R. W. Davies *Soviet History in the Gorbachev Revolution*, Bloomington: Indiana University Press, 1989.

Robert Ehlers, *et al.* (eds.), *The USSR Today: Perspectives from the Soviet Press*, 7th edn, Columbus, OH: Current Digest of the Soviet Press, 1988.

Viktor Bozhovich (ed.), *Repentance* [*Pokaianie*], Moscow: 1988 [in Russian].

For Western scholarly and critical responses:

Julie Christensen 'Tengiz Abuladze's *Repentance* and the Georgian Nationalist Cause', *Slavic Review* Vol. 50, no. 1 (Spring 1991), pp. 163–75.

Peter G. Christensen 'Tengiz Abuladze's *Repentance*: Despair in the Age of Perestroika', *Soviet and East European Drama, Theatre, and Film* Vol. 8, nos 2–3 (December 1988), pp. 64–72.

Janet Maslin '*Repentance*: A Satire from Soviet' [sic], *New York Times*, 4 December 1987.

Karen Rosenberg 'The Movies in the Soviet Union', *The Nation* (21 November 1988).

Josephine Woll 'Soviet Cinema: A Day of Repentance', *Dissent* Vol. 35, no. 2 (Spring 1988), pp. 167–9.

Denise J. Youngblood '*Repentance*: Stalinist Terror and the Realism of Surrealism', in Robert A. Rosenstone, (ed.) *Revisioning History: Film and the Construction of a New Past*, Princeton Studies in Culture/Power/History, Princeton, NJ: Princeton University Press, 1995, pp. 139–54.

Further Viewing

'Fiction' Films from the Eighties about the Stalin Era:

The Cold Summer of 53 [*Kholodnoe leto piatdesiat tret ego*], dir. Aleksandr
Proshkin, 1988.
Defense Counsel Sedov [*Zashchitnik Sedov*], dir. Evgenii Tsimbal, 1989.
Freeze, Die, Come to Life [*Zamri, umri, voskresni*], dir. Vitalii Kanevskii, 1989.
My Friend Ivan Lapshin [*Moi drug Ivan Lapshin*], dir. Aleksei German, 1983,
rel. 1985.

Documentaries from the Eighties about the Stalin Era:

I Served in Stalin s Guard [*Ia sluzhil v okhrane Stalina*], dir. Semen Aranovich,
1989.
Is Stalin with Us? [*Stalin s nami?*], dir. Tofik Shakhverdiev, 1989.
Solovki Power [*Vlast solovetskaia*], dir. Marina Goldovskaya, 1988.